ON BEING A JEWISH CHRISTIAN

Also by Hugh Montefiore

Oh God, What Next?

On Being a Jewish Christian

Its Blessings and its Problems

Hugh Montefiore

Hodder & Stoughton
LONDON SYDNEY AUCKLAND

British Library Cataloguing in Publication Data
A record for this book is available from the British Library

ISBN 0 340 71377 1

Typeset by Avon Dataset Ltd, Bidford-on-Avon, Warks

Printed and bound in Great Britain by
Mackays of Chatham PLC, Chatham, Kent

Hodder and Stoughton
A division of Hodder Headline PLC
338 Euston Road
London NW1 3BH

This book is dedicated to all, Jews and Christians,
who have helped me on my way

Contents

Preface

This book takes its origin from a suggestion by Owen Chadwick that I write something about Christians and Jews. Although I am born a Jew and I have been a Christian for over half a century, I have always kept off this particular subject because I thought that it would do more harm than good. Gentiles are not really interested. Jews, I felt, would be the last people to welcome anything by a Jewish Christian, even if they could swallow such a phrase without choking.

I changed my mind after I read Rabbi Julia Neuberger's book *On Being Jewish*. Much as I admire and like her, I found some things in her book with which I disagreed, and I thought to myself 'Why not a book *On being a Jewish Christian*'? I am too old now to cause trouble, and perhaps such a book needs to be written because Christians seem to ignore the fact that there are any Jewish Christians at all, which is very odd when one considers that Jesus was a Jew and the first Christians were all Jewish Christians, and there are quite a number of us still.

The position of Jewish Christians has greatly improved. In 1925 the President of the International Committee of the Hebrew Christian Alliance said: 'We are a twice despised and twice exiled people – exiled along with the Jewish race, and exiled *from* the Jewish race because of our belief; despised like the Jewish race, but despised *by* the Jewish race because of our belief' (Levison, 1925). This is certainly not the case today. But Christians still suppose that the Church of God consists exclusively of Gentiles, which isn't true; and even if it were true, it oughtn't to be the case, because Christianity is a universal religion or it is nothing.

So I decided to write this book. After all, I am Jewish, I feel Jewish, and I love the race to which I belong. Becoming a Christian has in no way diminished that love, nor has being a Jew diminished my love of Jesus Christ. As for the Jewish religion, there are aspects of this that I actually prefer to the Christian religion, especially parts of its liturgy. The Christian faith still has much to learn from Judaism, and – may I say it? – vice versa. In the pages that follow I shall attempt to explain myself; and this will include explaining Jews and Judaism to Gentiles, and looking at their past history, because otherwise it is not possible to know what it means to be a Jewish Christian. I do not imagine that what I write will be popular. Many Jews will not like it, because I am a Christian and so in a sense a traitor. Many Christians will not like it because I have strong criticisms of the Christian Church. Messianic Jews will not like it, because I do not count myself among their number. But then I do not seek to be popular. I only want to be understood. If some chapters of this book are written more passionately than usual, that is because they are about matters which mean so much to me.

I am grateful for help from John Fieldsend, Ian Kitteringham and Maurice Wiles, and especially to Marcus Braybrooke and Andrew White, who have looked through my manuscript and made helpful suggestions; but of course, I alone am responsible for what I have written.

Hugh Montefiore

I

On being Jewish

I was born into a Jewish family, and it didn't take me many years to find this out. How did I know I was Jewish? Not because I was circumcised! After all, this had happened on the eighth day after my birth, and so I naturally carried no memory of this painful occasion. In fact, I did not realise that I was different in this respect from most of the Gentile world until I was sent away to a preparatory school some nine years later.

How then did I realise that I was Jewish? It was just in the air. There was talk about Jewish friends, Jewish cousins, Jewish forebears. Pork or rabbit never made its appearance on the table. For one week in the year there was no bread: instead we had a kind of biscuit (during Passover) called *matzah*. When I was taught to say my prayers, my mother got me to say by heart one or two of the Hebrew psalms. On Friday evenings my father took a short service of Kiddush before the evening meal, with bread and wine, for the sanctification of the Sabbath. Saturday, not Sunday, was the family holy day. These little outward things impressed me as a little boy, especially matters of food. On the Day of Atonement for example, after fasting all day (except that as a small boy I wasn't allowed to), we would come home to an enormous spread of cold fried fish, and it was *delicious*.

It was only much later that I came to find out that so far as genealogies can go, I am entirely Jewish by blood (or as one ought to say nowadays, by genes). I can trace back my forebears on the

Montefiore side to fifteenth-century Italy, and on my mother's side there were Jewish de Passes in Spain right back at the time of the Inquisition and before that. Naturally, when I grew up, I was very proud of that inheritance. But as a child I had all this to learn. I even had to learn that I had a Jewish name as well as an English one, Adam ben Mordecai.

From the practices of adult Jewry I was more or less sheltered in my very young days, because I was, alas, brought up in a household where (apart from the holidays) I was pretty well confined to the nursery. My Nanny was not Jewish, so she couldn't explain Judaism to me. But she consorted in Kensington Gardens, where we went for walks, with the nannies of other Jewish boys and girls, and so even at that early stage I was brought up among Jews. As I began to grow up, it dawned on me that we saw a lot of our relations and family friends, who were all Jewish, and I hardly came across non-Jews until I went to my first school.

I began to learn about my Jewish heritage. Early on I was taught the stories from the Bible about the heroes of the past: Abraham, Moses, David, Solomon and the rest. For Christians the canonical prophets are the most important people of the Old Testament; but not really for most Jews. Moses and his Torah (Law) come first. Of course I never used the words 'Old Testament'. It is a phrase which only Christians use in their 'takeover' of the Jewish Bible. So far as I was concerned, the Bible was simply the books of what Christians call the Old Testament, and it never occurred to me that there were any more books in the Bible than those.

We were a Sephardi family, and so we worshipped at the Spanish and Portuguese Sephardi Church in Lauderdale Road, North London. The original Sephardi synagogue (and the earliest synagogue to be built after the Jews were allowed back in England in the time of Oliver Cromwell) was Bevis Marks. Although it has been enlarged and rebuilt, this graceful synagogue still stands in the City of London, but as my family was living in West London it was too far for us to travel, and even the Lauderdale Road Synagogue was more than a Sabbath day's journey away from us, and so we drove there, leaving our car a few hundred yards from the building.

We were moderately strict in our observance of the Jewish food taboos. We kept off the forbidden birds and animals vetoed in the Bible, eating only fish with fins and scales, and no animals that did not have the cloven hoof. But we did not engage in the complex ritual cleansing required later by the rabbis. We tended to keep to biblical rather than to rabbinical norms. In a sense we were rather like the Karaites, a Jewish sect which recognises the regulations of the Bible, but not of the Talmud. Not that we were members of the Liberal Jewish movement, which disregards the food laws. It was more a matter, I suspect, of partial assimilation to English mores. We were distinct from non-Jews in that we kept to the basic vetoes, but as an English family we did not distance ourselves too much from the English ethos, which was as much a part of our inheritance as our Jewish culture.

Perhaps I had better explain about the Sephardim. Their known origin is Spain (which is what the word means), from which they were exiled by Ferdinand and Isabella just over four hundred years ago. Many went to the Low Countries (from which some came to England) and to Eastern Europe via Turkey, where the Muslim regime welcomed them after their exile from Christian lands. They were of the same tradition as the many Jews of North Africa and the Yemen, almost all of whom have now emigrated to Israel or to the United States.

The other large Jewish grouping is the Ashkenazim. They found their way in large numbers to Germany, Poland and Russia. A great many Ashkenazim came to England after the Russian pogroms at the end of the First World War, and more stayed here or passed through England during the Nazi period in Germany. They arrived in England in a penniless condition long after the Sephardim had been established for some centuries and in some comfort in these islands. Although the Sephardim did much to alleviate Ashkenazi poverty (through the Jewish Board of Guardians), they regarded themselves on the whole as rather superior, although the position has now changed. It was a situation not unlike the way in which Anglicans regarded Methodists in the last century, or old English recusant families thought of immigrant Irish labourers who were also Roman Catholics.

No one knows how Sephardim and Ashkenazim originally came into being. Some think that, after the destruction of the Jewish Temple in AD 70, many Jews left Palestine, those in the north going north, and those from the south going west, the former becoming Ashkenazim in central Europe, and the latter Sephardim. Some think that the Sephardim derive from Babylonia, which was a main focus of Jewry in the early centuries AD. No doubt political and social conditions played their part in their differentiation. The pronunciation of Hebrew is different between the two groups. Even their alphabets and writing differ, and also their liturgies and customs. The differences although marked had little religious significance, and were rather the expression of the differing cultures of the two groups. Sephardim are probably more pure-blooded Jews than many who regard themselves as Ashkenazim. This is because in the eighth century AD the Khazar Empire, wedged between Christian Russia and the Arab Islamic Empire, opted to become Jewish. The whole nation converted. Uncomfortable as it may be for Ashkenazim, in Russia and Eastern Europe most Jews there probably inherit Khazar rather than Semitic blood. In fact, the hooked nose said to be characteristic of Jews stems not from the Middle East, but from Khazar origins (Koestler, 1976).

Nowadays Ashkenazim greatly outnumber Sephardim in England. Many of the customs which are associated with Judaism are in fact derived from Eastern European culture, and the same applies to what are regarded as typically Jewish dishes. These were not our customs as Sephardim. We didn't wear skull caps (although men do wear the prayer shawl or *taleth* in synagogue). Our delicacies do not include chopped liver or those rather delicious potato cakes you used to be able to get at Bloom's restaurant in the East End of London. Sephardim do not wear long side-burns and dress in black with those long droopy black hats. I'm afraid that Sephardim are so assimilated to British culture that they do not have any obvious points of difference from non-Jewish English people.

I remember most vividly the Jewish feasts of my childhood, and it may be helpful to recall them. As another contemporary Jewish

Christian has written about bringing up her child:

> I found myself telling her about my own struggle to live
> Christianity the Jewish way, finding God in the mundane events
> of every day, at home, in food, festivals, symbols. And it occurred
> to me that this might be an important dimension for a Church
> which in recent years has been exploring new ways of communi-
> cating with God, rediscovering meditation and the mediaeval,
> mystical and even Celtic tradition. What, if in its search for
> spirituality, it was to go further back, to its roots? Human beings
> who don't know their roots have a sense of disorientation.
> Christians without a feel for Judaism flounder a little in the
> entirely Jewish world of the New Testament. (Guinness, 1994)

Passover was always fun. We often went away to my widowed aunt,
whose husband (killed in the First World War) would have been
head of the family. Passover is a memorial of the escape of the Jews
from the slavery of Egypt, as described in the Book of Exodus, and
of course this has a more contemporary meaning, as Jews since
then have so often been in near-slavery conditions. The head of the
household takes the service – but it is a meal with a service, rather
than the other way round, like worship with some food and drink
afterwards, as can happen in a Christian parish.

There are bitter herbs, to remind us of the bitterness of Egypt.
There are *matzoth*, or unleavened bread, to remind us that the Jews
left Egypt with no time to bake leavened bread. (Scholars tell us
that this was really a relic of the spring harvest festival which
Passover supplanted, but what does that matter?) There was the
shankbone of the shoulder of a lamb, in commemoration of the
Passover lamb which was killed and its blood put on the doorpost
of the Jews' houses in Egypt, so that the angel of God 'passed over'
their houses in carrying out the last of the ten plagues, the death of
the Egyptian first-born. (The Samaritans, of whom only about a
thousand are left, still roast their Passover lamb on spits on Mount
Gerizim, and I have watched them do it; and the Greek Orthodox
do the same on Easter Day.) There is an egg, roasted on the coals, as

a reminder of the offering formerly brought to the Temple in Jerusalem on the festival. There are *haroset*, made from almonds, apples and other fruits, to remind us of the lime and mortar with which the Jews made bricks for Pharaoh in ancient Egypt. And of course there was quite a family feast. All this was rather fun.

There were four cups of wine to be drunk. There were also three large matzah cakes, and one of them is known as the *afikomen*. I remember later, when I was a don in Cambridge, Dr Daube reading a learned paper in which he suggested that this is really a loan word from the Greek, *aphikomenos*, 'he who could come', symbolic for the Messiah, who has been expected to come at Passover. Not that we laid a place for him, but there *was* always one vacant chair, and that was kept for the prophet Elijah, whom we are told in the last chapter of the Hebrew Bible would return to earth in the last days. We ended by singing the *Hallel*, that is to say a collection of joyful psalms, although I am afraid that my family were so tone deaf that it must have sounded a terrible cacophany to any outsider. (Incidentally outsiders are invited to this Seder service, and it has been a great pleasure to me to have come back to it on occasions with some of my family after my retirement.)

There were other matters of interest in the service, especially for the young. I remember clearly, all those years ago, being once the youngest person present and so having to say the *Manishtanah* – 'Why is this night different from all other nights . . . ?' – which was then answered by the head of the household. As all the service was in Hebrew, saying the *Manishtanah* involved quite a lot of homework beforehand for a six-year-old! Another special characteristic of the service was the way we all sat. 'Why on all other nights do we eat and drink, in a sitting or leaning position, but on this night we all lean?' (Answer: because we are free from the slavery of Egypt.) We were always amused when we came to that part of the service where we are told that 'Ribbi Eliezer, Ribbi Joshua, Ribbi Eliezer the son of Azariah, Ribbi Akiba, Ribbi Tarfon gathered at a Passover meal continued discussing the departure from Egypt all night until their disciples came and said "Rabbis, the time has come for the morning Shema" ' ('Hear O Israel . . .', said by Jews as Christians

6

say the Lord's Prayer). We were allowed to stay up late, but not as late as that! My brother always got the giggles when we reached that part of the service when we were told how Rabbi Akiba calculated by a remarkable sleight of hand that there were not ten plagues but two hundred and fifty, and I used to like the way Rabbi Judah remembered what the Ten Plagues of Egypt were by means of a mnemonic which went (in Hebrew of course): 'The scorpion stung the uncle.'

We always had something special at the end of the Passover service, an extract from the diaries of Sir Moses Montefiore, our ancestor, whom no one has heard of now, but about whom everybody knew in Victorian times, being greatly respected as a benefactor and regarded as a roving ambassador for persecuted Jews in various parts of the world. (He even went twice to Russia in a coach and four to tell the Czar to stop his pogroms.) It was customary for each person to keep as a talisman a small piece of the one large Passover matzah, and on one occasion, when Moses and his wife Judith were sailing in the Mediterranean, making one of their many pilgrimages to the Holy Land, a terrible storm blew up; and when, after an intermission, it was about to blow up a second time, they all but despaired of life.

At this awful pause a little before noon, I threw into the sea a small piece of my last years' Passover cake to be laid by on the evening of the Agada, supplicating the Almighty to protect us to avert the coming tempest, likewise to tranquillise the still troubled ocean . . . Between seven and eight o'clock in the evening. It is with the warmest gratitude I humbly acknowledge and bear witness to the Almighty's kind interposition on our behalf. The clouds which appeared to every man on board so dreadfully threatening during the morning have by a miracle dispersed . . .'

Yes, I used to keep a piece of the matzah, although fortunately I never had occasion to use it like that.

I have described Passover in some detail because it is really the chief festival. Tabernacles also was fun. As the word suggests, it was the Feast of Booths, *Succoth*. According to Leviticus, 'ye shall dwell in booths for seven days, that your generations may know that I made the children of Israel to dwell in booths, when I brought them out of Egypt.' It was a remembrance of the forty years of wilderness wanderings. Not that we did dwell in booths for seven days, but we did have a *succah* built in the garden. Tabernacles was also the 'Feast of the Ingathering', the Jews' Harvest Festival, and on the festival we would wave the *lulab*, which consisted 'the four agricultural species', that is branches of the palm tree, myrtle and willow, and also a lemon, and we would wave it around during the synagogue service. Great fun compared with merely solemnly holding up palm crosses on Palm Sunday.

And then there was *Hanuccah*, the commemoration of the famous Hasmonean family of the Maccabees who challenged the might of the powerful Seleucid dynasty in Syria which tried to veto Jewish customs and to enforce Greek culture in the Holy Land. They captured the Jewish Temple and defiled it for three years, but the Maccabees actually succeeded in recapturing it. According to the Talmud,

> when the Hasmoneans prevailed against the Greeks, they made search in the Temple and found only one cruse of oil which lay there untouched and intact with the seal of the High Priest. This cruse contained sufficient oil for one day's lighting only; but a miracle was wrought therein, and they lit the lamp with it for eight days. The following year these days were appointed a Festival with the reciting of the *Hallel* and thanksgiving.

We always used to light the Hanuccah lamps, starting with the lamp on the right, and on each succeeding day lighting also the next one until after eight days they were all lit. It was rather like the lighting of Advent Candles, except that we had some prayers. Hanuccah always falls near Christmas, and strict Jews give each other 'Hanuccah presents' instead of Christmas presents. I'm afraid we gave each other Christmas presents, and in the same way we enjoyed a conventional Christmas lunch. I suppose this represented the extent to which we had been affected by British culture. At the same time I never connected Christmas with the Christian Christ. It just never occurred to me that there was any connection. I suspect it is the same today with many people in our very secularised society.

There was also *Purim*. a word which means 'Lots', which recalls the lots which, according to the Book of Esther, were cast by Haman, in the reign of Ahasuerus King of Persia, in order to determine the best day for the execution of his evil plans to exterminate the Jews. The eve of the festival, 13 Adar, was the day appointed but Queen Esther, who was a Jewess but who had not disclosed her faith, called on her co-religionists to fast with her, and averted the evil decree. The story as told in the Bible seems most improbable, and Ahasuerus is unheard of elsewhere. What matter? Like the Book of Daniel, the Book of Esther was probably written to encourage Jews to hold fast to their faith in difficult times. It is interesting to note how many Jewish festivals are about the deliverance of the Jews from disaster; not only Purim, but also Passover and Hanuccah.

I used to enjoy the blowing of the *shofar* in synagogue on *Rosh Hashana*, the Jewish New Year's Day. (The Jewish calendar is a nightmare, with two New Years, days beginning at sunset the night before, and because the calendar was regulated by the moon and not the sun, a complete leap month was at times required: I never quite mastered it. I found it much more difficult than determining the date of Easter (later on in my life) by the use of the Golden Number in the old Prayer Book!) The *shofar* was a kind of trumpet made from a ram's horn, and doubtless needed some skill to make the right sounds. There were three notes, *tekiah* (sustained blast), *shevarim* (a succession of three notes) and *teruah* (a succession of short trills). I can still hear its sounds, over half a century later, reverberating in my ears.

We normally went to synagogue on a Saturday, but if we didn't go, we usually had a family service at home (I remember these because in solemn moments of prayer the shape of my father's head seemed to change and become more rounded, a phenomenon that fascinated me). In synagogue the ladies were upstairs in the gallery, and so could not participate much in the ritual, and I am told a good deal of gossiping took place up there. Downstairs the men all wore a *taleth*; and of course they kept their hats on all the time. They used to posh themselves up for the synagogue worship which we attended, the men in morning coats and top hats, rather like traditional old-fashioned German Lutheran pastors. I was riveted by the spats which one member always wore!

I think that Gentiles would be rather shocked by the amount of private conversation that would take place during Morning Service, which went on for a long time. There was quite a bit of congregational intervention, because whenever the name of the Lord was mentioned, people would say *Baruch who oubaruch shemo* (Blessed is He, and blessed is His name) in rather the same way as Charismatics nowadays tend to shout out 'Halleluiah' during a service of worship. There was always some ritual, especially when the *Sepher Torah* (scroll of the Law) was taken out of the 'ark' (where it was usually kept) and carried ceremonially on someone's shoulder (rather like a rifle), and taken to the *tebah*, the raised reading desk. As it passed by them, worshippers would touch it with their *taleth*. In the *tebah* it was stripped of its covering and ornaments to reveal the words of the first five books of the Bible (the Pentateuch) written in columns on a scroll of leather parchment wound round two metal holders. (One of the jobs I could do as a junior was to help unwrap the Torah when it reached the *tebah*: there were small bells on the top, a luscious embroidered covering, and the parchment wound round with cloth straps.) A strong man then lifted it up above his head, and displayed it to the four points of the compass, to the accompaniment of joyous chanting. I loved that. On a special occasion, at the Rejoicing of the Law, all the *sepher torah*s were carried ceremonially round the synagogue to great rejoicing.

Although there was also a *haftorah* (a reading from the prophets, chanted by a layman) the reading from the Books of Moses in the Torah was always chanted by the Minister. The *Mahammad* (the equivalent of the Parochial Church Council) sat in seats in the front of the *tebah*, and the presiding members arranged for people to be 'called up' to the *tebah* to attend successive portions of the day's reading. The first person to be called up was always a Cohen (that is, a member of a priestly family), followed by a Levite (from which the surname Levy of course is derived).

At the age of thirteen a boy is *barmitzvah*, which means that he has to take on all the duties (*mitzvot*) of an adult. In order to celebrate this occasion he has himself to chant one of the portions of the day's reading normally chanted by the minister. As the Hebrew writing is without vowels, he has to learn it very thoroughly (and those who do not know Hebrew have been known to learn the whole passage by heart). This is a terrible ordeal for any boy, and especially for someone like me who, in common with most of my family, am almost tone deaf. (Later on even the great Sir David Willcocks gave up in despair trying to make me sing in tune the versicles of Morning and Evening Prayer.) I was coached for the occasion by the minister, who looked (and was descended from) a Spanish grandee, with large mustachios and a very courteous bearing, the Revd David Bueno de Mesquita. He also made clear to me what my duties were as a Jewish adult. Then, after the service, there was a great feast at home, and the barmitzvah boy received lots and lots of the presents, some of which I still have.

These Jewish feasts and festivals remain vivid in my memory over half a century later. But Judaism is not primarily a religion reserved for times of worship. It is meant to permeate all life, and it is, in contrast to contemporary Christianity, a religion of the home rather than of the place of worship. There is a sense in which a father is priest to his family. Grace after meat is, so far as I know, never said in Christian households, and indeed the only time I have ever heard it in Christian England is in the perfunctory 'Benedicto benedicatur' muttered after Oxbridge High Table meals (sometimes caricatured as 'Benedictine benedecanter'). But in Jewish households there is a long thanksgiving extending for five pages in my Hebrew prayer book. We had it on special occasions. I remember 'mugging it up' so that I was reasonably fluent in the Hebrew when I was in my teens.

Of course, I was taught as a child to say my prayers – in English!

It was not just the 'God bless Mummy and Daddy . . .' variety. We always said the *Shema*' (Deut. 6: 4–9), the Jewish prayer which holds the place for Jews that the Lord's Prayer does for Christians:

Hear O Israel, the Lord is our God! The Lord is one! (Blessed be the name of his glorious kingdom for ever and ever!) And thou shalt love the Lord thy God with all thy heart, and with all thy soul and with all thy might. And these words which I command thee this day shall be in thy heart. And thou shalt teach them diligently to thy children, and shalt speak of them when thou sittest in thy house, and when thou walkest by the way; when thou liest down and when thou risest up. And thou shalt bind them for a sign upon thine hand; and they shall be for frontlets between thine eyes. And thou shalt write them on the posts of thy house and upon thy gates.

We did not use phylacteries on the hands and face as prescribed in this prayer: only very Orthodox Jews do that. But we did have *mezuzoth* – little metal cylinders containing Deuteronomy 6: 4–9 and Deuteronomy 11: 13–21 (a kind of secondary *Shema*'). You can't actually see the texts, as they are inside a little container, only about two or three inches high, painted in the same colour as the door frame, so that the Hebrew within is completely invisible. But still, if you look carefully at most Jewish houses, you will find them.

When I was young, before I went to school, I had lessons from a Miss Manville, who seemed to teach most of those whom Chaim Bermant has called (I dare not write christened) 'The Cousinhood', referring to the leading Anglo-Jewish families of the time, who usually intermarried. Miss Manville taught me the stories of the Hebrew Bible, and a smattering of Jewish history (although she omitted the nasty bits about anti-Semitism, which meant that she omitted a very great deal).

I did not receive regular Jewish religious instruction until I went to Rugby School. I did not attend church worship at the residential preparatory school to which I went (I rather enjoyed being left behind in an empty school building when all the others went to

Church on Sundays); and when I went to Rugby School, I also did not attend chapel (I had never even entered the building) and I absented myself from the RE lessons (I think I attended house prayers in the evening, although I cannot remember doing so at that stage). But the Rugby authorities sensibly made a rule that if a boy was to be excused chapel services (and these took place every weekday and at least twice on Sundays) and did not attend the religious education provided by the school, his parents must provide alternatives. My father, at great expense, hired someone who spent the Saturday night in a Rugby hotel and who gave me and another boy a lesson each Sunday morning when everyone was in chapel. In that way I began to learn quite a bit not only about the Bible, but about the Mishnah and the Talmud (which contain later interpretations of biblical law) and also about Jewish religious history and thought.

I took it all quite seriously and at the age of 15 and 16 I even thought of becoming a rabbi when I grew up, although I soon discarded the idea, partly because it seemed to me that the minister was very much at the beck and call of his congregation (rather as are some Free Church ministers) and partly because at that stage Jewish ministers of religion were really interpreters of Jewish Law, and did not have pastoral duties (although nowadays they are generally considered as pastors); and I did not care for that. It was not customary then for members of the congregation to invite the rabbi to the house, and he was not expected to call. He was there to take the services and to interpret the Torah as needed.

And then for me it all changed.

At the age of 16, sitting in my study one afternoon, and indulging in an adolescent muse, I saw clearly a figure in white (although the figure was and is still clear in my memory, I would doubt if it would have shown up on a photograph). Although I had never even read the New Testament, or attended a Christian service of worship, I knew immediately that the figure was Jesus, and I heard the words 'Follow me'. And that is what I have (not all that successfully) tried to do. Many explanations of such visions of Jesus have been attempted (Wiebe, 1997), but, so far as I am concerned, it was an incursion of the Transcendent into my life. (I am told on good authority that 60 per cent of all Messianic Jews in Israel were never evangelised, but, like me, had a vision or something similar.)

My conversion was as simple and as momentous as that. But it never occurred to me that by doing so I was negating my previous religious experience, and my earlier religious practice. That was as much an authentic part of myself as my Christian experience, and so it has remained. In the morning I was a Jew, and by the evening I was a Christian; not just a Christian but a Jewish Christian.

2

Jewry and Christendom

I have tried to recount as accurately as I can my memories of being Jewish during the first sixteen years of my life. After I became a Christian as a result of my conversion experience it was hardly surprising that I found myself cut off from the Jewish community, except for my immediate family of parents and two brothers (and even my relationships with my brothers were at times not all that easy). Although I was a bit lonely as a result of this, I cannot with hindsight blame anyone in any way. For a Jew to become a Christian is to go over to the enemy.

Most Jews do not know in detail the horrific story of the ways in which Christians from their positions of power have treated the Jewish people down the ages. (Still less are Christians aware of this terrible story.) But although Jews may lack precise knowledge of what has happened, they inherit a folk memory of the way in which the Jewish people have been treated. From their point of view for a Jew to become a Christian is for him to identify himself with a religion whose adherents have for centuries and centuries conceived an implacable hatred or dislike of their race, and for which they have never apologised. In past centuries a few Jews have converted in order to escape persecution or for their own personal advancement. This, although treacherous, was at least understandable. But for a Jew to embrace Christianity for no ulterior motive other than his own convictions is, for most practising Jews, both damnable and incomprehensible. (Orthodox Jews regard a

Jewish convert to Christianity as ceasing to be a Jew, and undergo a period of mourning as they would for someone who has died.) How could a person conscientiously embrace a Church which claims to be based on love when it has treated the Jewish race with such hatred? This book is about my being a Jewish Christian, but it is impossible to understand what this means without examining the attitude of Christians towards Jews, and this involves a consideration of their relations down the centuries. In order to attempt this, we must go right back to the beginning.

The New Testament

Christians were originally a sect of the Jews. They began by worshipping with their fellow Jews in the Temple in Jerusalem. Soon the Christian movement spread outside the Holy Land among the Jews dispersed around the Mediterranean, aided no doubt by those Jews from the Diaspora who were in Jerusalem for the festival of Pentecost and who witnessed the charismatic outburst which marked the start of the Christian movement. They then later heard Peter address them and it is said that three thousand of them became Christians on that day. (There are said to have been some eight million Jews at that period, and more of them lived outside the Holy Land than in Palestine during the New Testament period. There were as many as sixty thousand in Rome itself.)

As the number of converts increased outside the Holy Land, non-Jews were drawn into their Christian fellowship, and there arose problems about whether these Gentile members of the Christian sect could be expected to keep all the commandments of the Jewish Law, as Jews had to do. According to Acts 15 the matter was so pressing that a special meeting of the church in Jerusalem was needed, as a result of which the Gentile Christians were dispensed from keeping Jewish ritual laws and required to keep only what seem like 'the Noachine commandments' required by Jews of 'God-fearers'. Although the Acts of the Apostles may well give a somewhat idealised account of the first non-Jewish adherents to Christianity, and the way in which their problems were solved, it is clear from the writings of St Paul that circumcision, required of every Jewish male child, was not required of these Gentile converts. This must have been an affront to observant Jews which would hardly make them warm to this new sect in their midst.

It has been rightly said that the seeds of Christian anti-Semitism are to be found in the New Testament itself, and for this reason we must examine three particular texts in some detail. The first is taken from a letter sent by St Paul to the church at Thessalonika in Greece which Paul himself had founded. He told the Christians there that Jesus Christ would be revealed from heaven with his mighty angels, 'in flaming fire taking vengeance on them that know not God, and that obey not the gospel of our Lord Jesus Christ, who shall be punished with everlasting destruction from the presence of the Lord and from the glory of his power' (2 Thess. 1:8). How is this passage to be explained? I think that we must say that in his letters to the Thessalonians, if he wrote them (the authorship of 2 Thessalonians has been contested by some), Paul was not at his best. The letters would have been written fairly early in his Christian discipleship, and a far more balanced reference to the Jewish people is to be found in his later Epistle to the Romans. Even for those people who may wish to ascribe infallibility to St Peter and his successors, the Bishops of Rome, there is no need to regard as infallible the angry outbursts of St Paul to the Thessalonians written in a letter in the heat of the moment.

The second text is to be found in St Matthew's Gospel. After Jesus had been arrested and handed over to Pontius Pilate the Roman governor, a 'multitude' of Jews gathered round him, and Pilate solemnly told them that he was 'innocent of the blood of this just person'. They responded with the terrible words: 'His blood be upon us and upon our children' (Matt. 25:27). We may take leave to doubt whether a multitude of Jews ever did confront Pilate. Any who were present certainly did not represent the whole Jewish race, nor did they say those awful words ascribed to them. They represent rather the violent feelings against the Jews felt by the Jewish Christian community to which the evangelist belonged;

and these feelings have been intruded into the Gospel narrative (J. Sanders, 1993). After all, there had been some killings and stonings of Christians by Jews, as recounted in the Acts of the Apostles and by Josephus, and no doubt feelings ran high as a result of the Jewish Christian claim that Jesus was the expected Messiah. James the Lord's brother, the leader of the Jerusalem church, was renowned as a strict Jew, but none the less he was martyred for his faith. But that is no excuse whatsoever for the addition of these appalling words in St Matthew's Gospel. I can sympathise with my Jewish cousin Claude Montefiore who in his commentary on the Synoptic Gospels (C. G. Montefiore, 1927) wrote on this verse:

> A terrible verse; a horrible invention. Note the bitter hatred which makes the Evangelist write *pas ho laos* (all the nation). The whole people is supposed to be present. Hence all the atrocities which Christian rulers and peoples, sometimes, it must be freely acknowledged, with the disapproval of the Church, have wrought upon the Jews were accepted, and invoked upon their own heads, by the Jews themselves. This is one of those phrases which has been responsible for oceans of human blood, and a ceaseless stream of misery and desolation.

In the third text under consideration, some even more terrible words are put into the mouth of Jesus himself according to St John's Gospel:

> If God were your Father, ye would love me: for I proceeded forth and came from God; neither came I of myself, but he sent me. Why do ye not understand my speech? Even because ye cannot hear my word. Ye are of your father the devil, and the lusts of your father ye will do. He was a murderer from the beginning, and abode not in the truth because there is no truth in him. (John 8:42–4)

It seems likely that here too later events have cast their shadow backwards on to the Gospel narrative. Jewish Christians were living side by side with Orthodox Jews. Evidence from ossuaries suggests that, at any rate in some cases, there was not as yet total apartheid, for occasionally Jewish Christians seem to have been buried in Jewish burial sites (J. Sanders, 1993). But there had been, as we have noted, occasional stonings and killings of Christians by Jews, who were doubtless enraged by what they regarded as blasphemous claims about Jesus of Nazareth. Around AD 80 a curse on heretics (aimed at Jewish Christians) was added by the Jews to the Eighteen Benedictions in their liturgy. This probably accounts for the use of the word *aposunagogos* (cast out of the synagogue) used three times in St John's Gospel. Emotions again had run very high, and the remark 'Ye are of your father the devil' probably reflects the feelings towards the Jews on the part of Jewish Christians during this period. They are not the words of Jesus himself. At this point the Jews were in a position of power, and the Christians felt themselves under attack, and, alas, they reacted with venom.

The early Church Fathers

Jerusalem fell to the Romans in AD 70. After this there remained Jewish Christians in the Holy Land, but we know little enough about them, and it is not impossible that their writings have been suppressed or distorted by the overwhelmingly Gentile Church outside the Holy Land, if these did not accord with later Christian orthodoxy. After the second Jewish revolt in AD 135, the city of Jerusalem was levelled to the ground, and a pagan city of Aelia Capitolina was built in its place, with the Temple of Jupiter standing on the site of the old Jewish Temple. Since Rabbi Akiba regarded Bar Cochba, the leader of the revolt, as the Jewish Messiah, Jewish Christians who knew that their Messiah had already come were sharply divided from their fellow-Jews in Palestine. We know nothing about Jewish Christianity after this in the Holy Land, but Christianity continued to spread like wildfire in the Mediterranean world, where there were already long established, large and thriving Jewish communities. Christian polemic against the Jews increased.

They were reprobate, their minds were darkened, they misinterpreted the Scriptures, they had rejected their own Messiah, they had been passed over in favour of the Christian Church which had inherited the promises given to the Jews by God. The destruction of the Temple was a sign of God's wrath against the Jewish race. The Jews, angered by these taunts, responded by accusing Mary of being pregnant with Jesus by a Roman soldier called Panthera.

Judaism was the rival of Christianity. Christians believed that God no longer favoured the Jews; but despite the destruction of their Temple and their alleged desertion by God, Jews in the Diaspora prospered. They shared the same high morality as Christians, but in contrast to the masses who had been semi-converted to Christianity, their Jewish devotion was deep-seated and sincere. There always had been (as there are today) some Jewish Christians, and in addition there were some Judaised Gentile Christians. They are mentioned in Colossians 2:16 for their scrupulosity over food and drink, and by their observation of new moon or Sabbath. In the middle of the second century we know from Justin Martyr that Jewish Christians who kept to their Jewish customs and laws were welcome in the Church, so long as they did not impose these on others; but such Jewish Christians were regarded as 'weak-minded'. There are a few references to them in the Jewish Talmud. Origen spoke of them, and in the fourth century they were known to Jerome and Epiphanius. We cannot be certain precisely who were the Ebionites and the Nazaraeans who are mentioned by the early Fathers: all we really know is that they were Jewish Christians, and the Ebionites did not accept the Virginal Conception of Jesus. The Quartodeciman controversy (whether Easter should be celebrated on 14 Nissan as the Christian Passover as happened in Asia, or on a Sunday as in the West) illustrates the difficulty the largely Gentile Church had in cutting itself off from the Jewish roots from which it had sprung. The Jewish date for Easter lasted in the East long after it had been prohibited by church councils.

In the fourth century a resurgence of Judaising Christianity took place. As a mark of their ownership of the Old Testament Scriptures,

Jewry and Christendom

the Jews read them in the original Hebrew, not in the Greek translations which the Christians used. Jewish festivals, the Jewish calendar, Jewish rituals, Jewish martyrs (the Church even adopted the Maccabean martyrs!) and, it must be added, Jewish magic, all had their peculiar attractions. These appealed to members of the Church, and not merely those who had been converted from Judaism. Their members began attending the synagogue as well as the church. The Church's spokesmen turned their invective against these Judaising Christians by vilifying the Jews. The best known of their preachers was John Chrysostom. In 386–7 in Antioch he preached eight sermons against the Jews and Judaising Christians. Although he was called 'golden mouthed' (*chrysostomos*) and achieved 'sainthood', so far as Jews were concerned he was un-believably foul mouthed. Although his sermons seem to have had very little effect (a century later another Christian preacher there faced a similar situation) his language was deplorable: 'They built themselves a brothel in Egypt, they made love madly with the barbarians and they worshipped foreign gods', he declared. In another passage he linked their sensuality with their rejection of God: 'As an animal when it had been fattened by getting all that it wants to eat, grows stubborn and hard to manage, so it was with the Jewish people. Reduced by gluttony and drunkenness to a state of utter depravity, they frisked about and would not accept Christ's yoke.'

The chief charge against the Jews was that they had had Jesus put to death. 'If someone had killed your son, could you stand the sight of him or the sound of his greeting? Wouldn't you try to get away from him as if he were an evil demon, as if he were the Devil himself?' Chrysostom even called the Jews 'deicides' (killers of God) because they had had Christ put to death. Hence their eternal punishment. 'It is because you killed Christ. It is because you stretched out your hand against the Lord. It is because you shed the precious blood, that there is now no restoration, no mercy any more and no defence.' Chrysostom inveighed against synagogues: 'A place where a whore stands on display is a whorehouse. What is more, the synagogue is not only a whorehouse but a theatre: it is also a den of thieves and a haunt of wild animals.' He alleges that demons haunt the souls of Jews. 'When animals are unfit for work, they are fit for slaughter, and this is the very thing that the Jews have experienced. By making themselves unfit for work, they have become ready for slaughter.'

An attempt has been recently made to whitewash Bishop John Chrysostom, which I find quite unconvincing (Wilken, 1983). John was following the Hellenistic tradition of rhetoric, like the three Cappadocians bishops, Basil, Gregory of Nyssa and Gregory Nazianzus. Before the days of the mass media, public speaking held the attention of the public. Making use of exaggeration, metaphor and comparisons, the particular form of rhetoric called the *psogos* consisted of unrelieved denigration, which John used against others as well as the Jews. He must be seen, we are told, in his historical context. Yes; but should not Christian leaders discard those pagan ways that led them into false allegations and unwarranted denigration? Do we not despise those preachers who, during the First World War, made use of popular prejudice in calling for a crusade against the despicable Boche and the hated Huns? Were not our laws against racialism introduced partly to prevent public speakers inciting hatred against Afro-Carribean immigrants by calling them dirty niggers? Christian preachers in the fourth century, if they had been true to their Christian calling, should have spoken with respect of their Jewish neighbours who lived alongside them in the cities of the ancient world.

In a largely Gentile Church, negative attitudes towards Judaising Christians rubbed off on Jewish Christians. The third century *Didascalia Apostolorum* warned against Jewish customs. The *Apostolic Constitutions* forbade Christians to enter synagogues. Even association with Jews by bishops and clergy involved deposition, and excommunication for a layman. Canon XXXVII of the Council of Laodicea (343–81) pronounced that it was not lawful to receive unleavened bread from the Jews or to be partakers of their impiety. Here is a later profession of faith from Constantinople:

I renounce all customs, rites, legalisms, unleavened breads and sacrifices of lambs of the Hebrews, and all other feasts of the Hebrews, sacrifices, prayers, aspersions, purifications, sanctifications and propitiations, and fasts, and new moons, and Sabbaths, and superstitions, and hymns and chants and observances and synagogues, and the food and drink of the Hebrews: in one word, I renounce absolutely everything Jewish, every law, rite and custom . . . (Parkes, 1934)

These regulations show how much difficulty the Gentile Church had in ridding itself of Jewish Christians and Judaising Christians. Even as late as AD 787, the Second Council of Nicea denounced those who 'secretly keep the Sabbath and observe other Jewish customs'. Jewish Christianity had been proscribed.

The main enemy, however, were the Jews. Christians believed that Jesus was the Christ, the Jews denied it; they could not both be right, and so the Jews were regarded as the opposition. Christians believed Jesus was divine, and so to Jews they were blasphemers. During these early centuries, many early Church Fathers revered by Christians, some of whom were even made saints, wrote theological treatises against the Jews, showing how the Jewish religion had been superseded by the Gentile Church. Tracts against the Jews were written, books of testimonies were compiled on texts from the Jewish Bible. Dialogues between Jews and Christians were composed, possibly based on actual confrontations, but written up with a heavy Christian bias. This suggests that there must have been quite a strong Jewish opposition against which these works were written. Sometimes the language was strong. For example, Eusebius, the famous church historian wrote that 'they would be utterly destroyed because of their sin against Christ' and that 'they would be dispersed throughout the whole world with never a hope of any cessation of evil or breathing space from troubles'.

This polemic against the Jews became stronger when the Roman Emperor Constantine the Great himself embraced Christianity. The Edict of Milan gave the persecuted Church freedom, and soon it became the established religion of the Empire. Christians felt free to deliver themselves against the Jews often with some violence. Many Christian Fathers wrote against the Jews. St Augustine for example said that they were unable to appreciate the spiritual nature of the Scriptures because they were incurably carnally minded. He also, with other Church Fathers, compared the Jews with Cain, destined to be a fugitive and wanderer on the earth, thus providing the prototype of the mediaeval myth of the Wandering Jew.

There was a respite when Julian the Apostate announced that he wanted to rebuild the Jewish Temple, thus encouraging not only Jews but also those Judaising Christians who were the precursors of today's Christian Zionists. But this respite was brief. The tables had been turned. Roles were reversed. Christians, not Jews, were now in a position of power, and they made horrible use of it against the Jews. The Roman Empire functioned on a slave economy, but Jews could no longer own Christian slaves. Thus they were eliminated from large-scale manufacture or agriculture. Christians could proselytise Jews, but Jews were forbidden to proselytise. Those who had been forced to become Christians were not allowed to return to their old religion. For a Christian man or woman to marry a Jew was a crime of adultery! Jews were excluded from holding any public office. They could no longer function as lawyers or judges. Their right to testify in court was subjected to increasing restrictions (Reuther, 1979). In AD 414 the Bishop of Antioch expelled all Jews from Alexandria, which had been the focus of Diaspora Jewry for over seven hundred years. There were especially ugly scenes, with pogroms and street fighting leading to the expulsion of Jews from all major cities. The Theodosian code was bad enough, according to which no Jew could exercise any authority over a Christian. The Justinian code was introduced in AD 534. It toughened restrictions and depressed their status still further. The Jewish Patriarch was no longer a publicly recognised dignitary, and the tax which Jews paid to him was diverted to the imperial coffers. The *fiscus Judaicus* which replaced the old Temple tax and which was originally imposed as a head tax on every Jew, was renewed.

Disability was gradually piled on disability. Although Jewish synagogues were protected by law (as indeed were Jews themselves), no more synagogues were permitted to be built. The date of the Jewish Passover had to be changed to ensure that it always came after the Christian Easter. Even in their own communities it was not permitted for Jews to read their Scriptures in Hebrew. Any Jew caught molesting a convert was liable to burnt at the stake.

It was not, however, wholly on account of their faith that Jews were hated. Way back in AD 38 there had been a terrible pogrom against the Jews of Alexandria, which was perhaps the largest city in the ancient world after Rome, and where there lived very large numbers of Jews. This pogrom had nothing to do with Christianity whatsoever. Jews were unpopular partly because they enjoyed in Alexandria special privileges from the imperial power, partly because they were wealthy, and partly because of their exclusiveness and religious intolerance and refusal of emperor worship. Their unpopularity increased after the Jewish revolts against Rome in AD 70 and AD 135. As a result of the murder and enslavement of most of the Jewish population in the Holy Land (the number of Jews overall dropped from eight million to one million between the first and tenth centuries AD), Jews were no longer farmers, but became urban dwellers, and very successful they were at commerce, with their international connections. Later, when the Arabs conquered Babylonia in the Dark Ages, the Jews lost their agricultural holdings there through high taxation, and they were forced into the cities. This did not increase their popularity.

At the same time the main cause of their unpopularity was the hatred engendered against them on Christian grounds. Christianity laid claim to the divinity of Christ. If Christ was divine, then Judaism must be false. Christianity had taken so much from Judaism, from which it derived, that it was this one great divide that separated the two faiths. In a sense they were in competition. If Christianity was to grow, it was necessary to show the falsity of Judaism, and since the Christians were in power, they made sure that Jews were very much second-class citizens.

The early Middle Ages

For some six hundred years, from the break up of the Western Roman Empire in the fifth century to the First Crusade at the end of the eleventh century, the Jews were able to live in comparative peace and without the oppressive restrictions that had been laid upon them by the imperial government (Küng, 1992). Many of them became wealthy and prosperous, and they spread throughout the then known world. It must be remembered that Jews lived by choice in the Jewish quarter of a city, where they felt more secure, and could practice their faith without offence to others. Walls were later built round their quarter for their own protection. It was not until the sixteenth century that legal restrictions were placed on Jewish settlements, and Jews, whose numbers were swollen by refugees, were forced to live in the *ghetto nuovo* in Venice (Küng, 1992).

Jews had lived in Italy since the days of the Roman Empire. Although we can't trace our family tree back beyond 1605, when Judah Leone Montefiore married one Rachel Olivetti, we can find Jews in one of the three Italian villages called Montefiore and they were engaged in banking right back in the fifteenth century. (At that time Jews did not have surnames and were known as, for example, Judah ben Mordecai (Judah the son of Mordecai). It looks as though the Montefiores are a leftover from the days of the Roman Empire rather than émigrés from Spain at the Inquisition. A branch came to England in the eighteenth century, and members of the family were later to be found in many parts of the Empire as well as in England.

The later Middle Ages

The attitude of Christians towards the Jews changed sharply at the beginning of the eleventh century, at the time of the First Crusade. A rumour had been spread that the Jews had warned the Sultan of Egypt that Christians were going to attempt to conquer his empire, which included Jerusalem. As a result the Jews became linked with the Muslims in the minds of Christian Europe. The first anti-Jewish riots (not sponsored by the authorities) took place during the First Crusade. No doubt greed and envy at Jewish wealth were partly the cause of these massacres. In the Holy Land there was a terrible slaughter by Crusaders of Jews (who were there allied to the Muslims), and only a very few survived. This anti-Jewish feeling meant that Jews were no longer able to use their connections for long-distance trading. They had been forced out of agriculture. There was little left to them other than moneylending and the keeping of local shops. Jews often became moneylenders. As Christians understood the Bible, they were forbidden to practice usury, but Jews, interpreting literally the biblical texts, were only forbidden to practice usury among their fellow Jews: it was permissible to lend money to Gentiles. Since Jews were so highly taxed, it is not surprising that they charged very high rates of interest; and this naturally did not endear them to their Gentile customers.

Worse was to come. Pope Gregory VII forbad them to undertake State offices, as they had been forbidden earlier under Roman imperial rule. Worse still, Pope Innocent III summoned the Fourth Lateran Council in 1215. It was decided that as all Jews were 'servants of sin', they should henceforth become the personal possession of Christian princes. They had to wear a special mark of identification on their dress, so that they could immediately be recognised. (In the Papal States this consisted of a red hat until one day a Jew was greeted mistakenly as cardinal of the Church, whereupon a yellow circle on the dress over the heart was prescribed.) They could not undertake any public office. They were not allowed out during Holy Week! They had to pay a special tax to Christian clergy! It is sad to relate that the new policy was enforced by the Dominican and Franciscan orders. The Church was triumphant over the Synagogue, which was depicted in some Gothic cathedrals as a woman in fetters with the tablets of the law falling from her hands. The Church had taken over the promises made to Israel, and the old Israel was left cowering in fear. All this from the adherents of a faith which proclaims that God is love!

During this period there were some religious dialogues arranged between Jews and Christians, but they were all set up by Christians, and the outcome was not in doubt. Usually the Church's spokesmen were Jewish Christian converts. One of the results of these dialogues was often that copies of the Talmud were ordered to be burnt, not for the first or the last time. It was not until 1686 that the first genuine dialogue between a Jew and a Christian took place (Schoeps, 1965).

Jews were already long established in the Yemen, North Africa, Spain, Italy, Germany and France, but it is hardly surprising that Jews who were suffering this terrible persecution tended to move to other parts. They made their way from the cities of the Rhine and the Danube into Central Germany, and later on to Poland, and to Russia and the Ukraine, where doubtless they mingled with the converts to Judaism from the old Khazar Empire. They took with them Yiddish, which is basically a mixture of Hebrew and Aramaic with High German. (There was a similar kind of mixture in Spain.) In England in 1190 there was a dreadful massacre at York, and there were further troubles for the Jews in 1255 through a wicked rumour that 'Little St Hugh' in Lincoln had been crucified 'as an insult to the name of Jesus' (Hyamson, 1928). After savage persecution, with many hangings and imprisonment and ruinous taxes, there was some respite, but after a papal bull on 'the accursed and perfidious Jews' addressed in 1282 to the Archbishops of Canterbury and York, their plight greatly worsened. They were finally expelled from England in 1290 from the seventeen towns to which they were then restricted. Some sixteen thousand left for France, Flanders and elsewhere. In Germany itself at that time, they fared a little better. They were under the special protection of the Emperor, and although they were cruelly taxed, they escaped other molestation.

Awful things happened in Spain. Under Moorish rule Jews had flourished. They were learned and cultured; doctors, lawyers, diplomats, officers in the army, in some respects the élite of the country. This was the heyday of Jewish culture. For a time under the Catholic conquerors of Spain, they still fared well, but as the reconquest of Spain was being completed, a terrible fate awaited them. The Inquisition was set up, as the word implies, to enquire into heresy, but in Spain the inquisitors were required to force Jews to be baptised, and those who refused were put to death. Jews were burned in their tens of thousands. In 1391 alone, twelve thousand forced baptisms took place in Valencia. The worst years of persecution were in the second half of the fifteenth century. After the recapture of Granada, the reconquest of Spain was completed, and Torquemada persuaded Ferdinand and Isabella in 1492 to face the Jews with either baptism or expulsion. This was an early attempt at a 'final solution'. Some hundred thousand left. Many went to Turkey and thence to those parts of the Turkish dominions which were in Eastern Europe. In the very year that they were expelled from Spain, some Jews set out under Columbus to discover the New World, where they have flourished ever since. But a great many Jews stayed in Spain and were baptised, although they secretly practised their Jewish faith. These were known as *marranos* (pigs). The Inquisition was kept very busy in dealing with them, bringing them to trial. Even St Teresa of Avila at one stage fell under suspicion.

At this point I have to declare an interest. My mother's family have the name of de Pass. They were Spanish Sephardi Jews who had obtained positions of eminence. De Pass is even one of the hereditary names of the Spanish royal family. There were de Pass poets and diplomats, and de Pass officers in the army. One Spanish de Pass was a diplomat sent to Rome and accredited to the Vatican. When it was found out in Spain that he had spent his time using his influence to persuade the Pope to stop confiscating the estates of 'new Christians' (i.e. Jews recently baptised), the Pope had to hide him for a time in a monastery. At the Inquisition, members of the family went to the Continent and spread across Europe and beyond, to France, Germany, Holland, Italy, Gibraltar, Martinique, Jamaica, and later to the USA, Australia and South Africa. They came to England around the time of Oliver Cromwell. They tended to be *marranos* as in 1633 the son of a wealthy merchant by the name of de Pass who professed Christianity came to England, but in 1683 his son was *barmitzvah* in Bevis Marks synagogue in London. Not all de Passes fared so well. One at least perished in the

Inquisition. Although he was known to have been baptised, he was heard to be reciting the *Shema'* as the flames engulfed his body. The fact that one of my ancestors was killed in the Inquisition has made a deep impression on me, and as a Christian I am very deeply ashamed of what my fellow Christians did to him, even if it took place over four hundred years ago.

Reformation times

Martin Luther began by being an advocate of the Jews. He attacked the many slanders about them, and disavowed the use of force against them. Later in his life however he changed his mind. Expectations of the imminent end of the world had fed the belief that before that happened there would be a mass conversion of Jews, and when that did not take place Luther, three years before his death, wrote a violently anti-Jewish pamphlet *On the Jews and Their Lies*. They were accused of arrogance, and the mediaeval slanders of well-poisoning and infanticide were repeated. He advocated the burning of synagogues, the destruction of houses, the confiscation of their Scriptures, the abolition of safe conducts, the confiscation of cash and jewelry, hard physical labour and expulsion from all Christian lands to Palestine. Fortunately his views were too extreme for the Emperor, who condemned the book; but later it provided wonderful material for Goebbels' attacks on the Jews and for Nazi propaganda. As for the other Reformers, Jews had already been banished from Zurich and Geneva, so Zwingli and Calvin did not especially inveigh against them, especially as these Reformers were not apocalypticists; but they suffered from the usual anti-Jewish prejudices of their time.

The Counter-Reformation was an attempt to reinstate ecclesiastical mediaevalism, so it is no surprise to find that there were also anti-Jewish Popes during this period. Paul IV exiled the Jews in Rome to a ghetto, and burned *Marranos*. Pius V issued an anti-Jewish bull which restricted Jewish settlements under his rule to two cities. Gregory VI also issued an anti-Jewish bull which extended the rights of the Inquisition against Jews, banned the Talmud, and ordered Jews in Rome to attend compulsory sermons.

It was not until near the end of the sixteenth century that Sixtus V revoked the expulsion of Jews, but a flourishing Jewish slave trade, centred in Malta, continued until the time of Napoleon. Jews were favoured as slaves because large sums of ransom moneys could be obtained.

Later developments

In 1643 Oliver Cromwell permitted the Jews to return to England, partly for economic reasons, partly due to a dearth of Hebrew scholars. But this did not presage a general thaw. There were massacres in the Polish Ukraine, a harbinger of later disasters to come. It was not until 1781 that Jews first gained equal rights, given by the enlightened Joseph II of Austria, the son of Maria Theresa. In 1789 the French Declaration of Human Rights brought liberty under the law to Jews within the French Empire, but the law could not eliminate anti-Jewish prejudices. After the defeat of Napoleon, the Congress of Vienna appeared to protect Jewish liberty, but this was a fudge. Some areas expelled Jews. Reaction set in. Only Holland in mainland Europe maintained the complete constitutional and legal equality which Jews had recently won. In 1819 in Germany Jews' blood was shed to the accompaniment of 'Hep, Hep, Hep' (the acronym for *Hierusolyma est perdita*, the watchword of the Crusades). None the less the position of the Jews gradually grew better, except for the Papal States in Italy. (It is hardly surprising that my Montefiore forebears had already moved from them to the freer atmosphere of Livorno.) There was a further reaction in Europe after the Franco-Prussian war. An anti-Semitic movement was born, to which Bismark lent his influence. As a result Jews in Germany, unless baptised, could not obtain an army commission or a university chair or any important office in the State. In France, the Dreyfus affair showed how deeply anti–Semitism was entrenched in the French army. These however were hiccups, and the onward tide of Jewish emancipation was unstoppable in Western Europe, except for the Papal States.

Here again I must declare an interest. In 1858 an officer of the papal police in Bologna removed from his Jewish parents their seven-year-old son Edgar Mortara on the grounds that a twelve-year-old servant girl had had him baptised at the age of two when the child was seriously ill, in order to save his soul. The boy was to be brought up as a Christian. The Emperor of Austria and the King of France advised Pius IX to yield, and at the behest of the Jewish Board of Deputies, Sir Moses Montefiore went out to try to persuade the Pope to allow the lad to be brought up as a Jew. Pio Nono would not even give him an audience (Roth, 1936). The decision about the boy was outrageous, absolutely contrary to human rights.

Eastern Europe and Russia

The situation in Eastern Europe was very different from that in Western Europe. There was virulent anti-Semitism in Romania. In Poland the position of the Jews had been deteriorating since the close of the Middle Ages. When the Jews there became part of the Russian Empire, it was the declared policy of the Czars to confine them to the newly acquired western provinces (known as 'The Pale of Settlement'). This involved the painful resettlement of some twenty thousand Jews. Then, under Czar Nicholas I, a further edict was issued that all Jews should be removed some thirty-five miles from the frontier with Austria and Germany. Once again I must declare an interest, for Sir Moses Montefiore in 1845 was invited to intervene and he went to see the Czar and actually persuaded him to abrogate the ukase. When the next Czar succeeded Nicholas, it looked as though a new age was dawning. But this was not to be. In 1881 a terrible pogrom against the Jews broke out, spreading like wildfire to one hundred and sixty cities, in which tens of thousands were massacred or left homeless. A second wave of persecution then broke over Warsaw, followed by an epidemic of arson. The Russian government tried to solve the problem by oppressing the victims. Jews were excluded from all villages even within the Pale of Settlement. They were subjected to appalling indignities (Jewish women were only allowed to live in the major cities if they wore the yellow ticket of a prostitute). No voice was raised against this by the Russian Orthodox Church, which always supported the secular authorities.

Little was done to assist the Jews who found themselves in a hopeless situation, on the verge of destitution. Their only hope lay in flight, and by the end of the century nearly a million Jews had left their homes to seek their future in a foreign land. Over a hundred thousand Russian Jews settled in the East End of London. Many more went to the USA.

After the First World War, the Russian Revolution fully emancipated Russian Jews, but it was disastrous to the continuance of Jewish life. Although Marx himself was Jewish (and likewise Trotsky), they were atheists. Synagogues were closed, Hebrew was frowned upon, public religious teaching was forbidden. Anti-Semitism was still rife among the people, as it still is today, with the connivance of the Russian Orthodox Church.

Anti-Semitism in modern times

Meanwhile in Europe twentieth-century anti-Semitism, while it was not obtrusive, usually lurked not far from the surface. I have to say that I was largely shielded from it, being brought up in a mainly Jewish milieu. It surfaced once at a day school I attended for a time in London, when I was branded with a red-hot poker above the knee on one occasion. I was young at the time, and I thought of it at the time as a case of bullying, and it was only later that I realised its anti-Semitic slant. Some residential schools had a restrictive quota for Jewish boys. I noticed the occasional anti-Semitic remark, and I took exception to the highly objectionable use of phrase 'Jewboy'. When people saw that I took offence, they would probably say: 'Of course I don't mean you', which somehow made it worse. Although it was not until the end of the nineteenth century that Jews enjoyed full equality, there are still golf clubs and luncheon clubs which do not elect Jewish members. Overt racialism can be circumvented by subtle systems of blackballing.

However all this is as nothing to what occurred in Germany.

Here horror was heaped upon horror, culminating in the attempted genocide of the whole Jewish race, with the murder of six million Jews carried out with cold efficiency. The *Diary of Anne Frank* and the film *Schindler's List* have brought all this alive for many. An eyewitness record is available (Wiesel, 1981) and the factual account of slave labour and genocide (Gilbert, 1986). It helps to see the Holocaust Museum in Jerusalem, if one wants to imagine the fears and sufferings of Jews, from France and the Netherlands to Hungary and Rumania, in fact throughout Nazi-occupied Europe. The events themselves are so horrendous that it almost diminishes their evil and fearfulness to describe them. This came home to me afresh when the wife of a German-born rabbi mentioned to me recently that she could not bear to go even today on a train in Germany (because it reawoke in her memories of Jews herded in cattle trucks drafted to extermination camps). I myself had little idea what was going on until after the war, as I was serving in the Army in the Far East, and I did not get home until after VE day. But earlier it was clear to me that terrible things were happening to Jews in Germany. My parents used to take in young boys who managed to get out of Germany, leaving their parents behind to die. We put them up until they left for Argentine or some other South American country, on their own of course. We knew about cruel persecutions, appalling indignities, and the shameless theft of Jewish possessions; but the Final Solution had not then begun.

The mass maltreatment of the Jews, ordered by Hitler, was not carried out simply by Nazis. Although there were heroic men and women, both Roman Catholic and Protestant, who risked their lives to save Jews (and Fr Maximilian Kolbe actually died in the place of a Jew), Christians as a whole did not raise their voices against what was happening or what they must have thought was happening: indeed, many co-operated (Goldhagen, 1997). The elimination and extermination of German Jewry had been advocated long before the Nazi terror. Virulent anti-Semitism had become deeply entrenched throughout Germany among both the laity and the leadership of the Protestant and Roman Catholic Churches. The Roman Catholic

Church kept silent before mounting evidence of maltreatment and murder. Between 1939 and 1945 the semi-official Vatican paper *Civilta Cattolica* published only two references to the Jews, both derogatory (Eckardt, 1986). As late as 1941 it wrote: 'The crime of the sons of the Synagogue has been repeated in every generation.' The Roman Church did not even move openly to the help of Jews in Rome. Even the 'Confessing Church' in Germany did not confront this issue but took its stand rather on 'purity of doctrine'. Pastor Martin Niemoller himself called the Jews 'alien and uncongenial' and described the fact that God revealed himself in the Jew Jesus of Nazareth as a 'painful and grievous stumbling block . . . to be accepted for the sake of the Gospel' (Gutteridge, 1976). Switzerland turned back Jews at its frontiers. But Denmark succeeded in evacuating seven thousand five hundred to Sweden as late as 1943. Rising anti-Semitism in the USA prevented raising their quotas of Jewish immigrants (Wyman, 1984). Britain admitted forty thousand in 1938. Vichy, despite its co-operation with the Nazis, offered Britain a thousand Jewish orphans in 1942: the offer, sadly, was refused. Yet it is said that the Allies (and in particular Jews) are not to be blamed for inaction in saving Jews from the Holocaust (Rubinstein, 1997). The Final Solution was not decided until 1942. The Allies certainly knew about it before the end of the war, but to disclose this would have revealed that they had cracked the German cypher which would have had disastrous consequences for the Allies.

The Holocaust could never have taken place had it not been for earlier anti-Judaism stoked up by the Christian churches, When on one occasion two bishops did come to confront Hitler on the issue of Nazi racial policy, he replied that he was only putting into effect what Christianity had preached and practised for nearly two thousand years. He was not wholly wrong. For example, the Nazis' Nuremberg laws had their prototype in the requirement of the Inquisition that those who wished to prosper in public life must prove that they had no hidden Jewish forebears, a requirement which still existed in Roman Catholic religious orders, such as the Jesuits, until the twentieth century (Reuther, 1979). Most of the foul anti-Semitic libels against the Jews had their protoype in earlier Christian anti-

Judaism. Whereas Christians did not exterminate the Jews (except in popular massacres) because they preferred to leave them as a living sign of rejection whom God would punish with hell, the Nazis took it upon themselves to carry out what Christians in earlier ages had decided to leave to God. Nazi anti-Semitism culminating in the Holocaust was a secularised form of Christian anti-Judaism.

Nor should it be supposed that anti-Semitism ended with the defeat of the Nazis. There are still attacks on Jewish synagogues and cemeteries. There are those today who propagate the monstrous lie that the Holocaust never took place (Harwood, nd). Racialism provides a useful scapegoat for those who feel themselves unfairly treated in life. Black and Asian people in the West now bear the brunt of most European racialism. But neo-Nazis have appeared, desecrating Jewish graveyards, and attempting to attack Jewish synagogues. Although this is all in a minor key compared with the past (and prohibited of course by law), it still exists.

Perhaps at this point it should be added that there may well be particular characteristics of some Jews which Gentiles find irritating or uncongenial. But it should be realised that a race which has been persecuted down the centuries is likely to be sharp-minded (for only the fittest could survive), that those whose forebears for centuries have been forced into usury or commerce are likely to be successful financiers or businessmen, and that insecurity and un-popularity tends to make people ostentatious or aggressive. It is hard to lay the blame for such characteristics on any Jews who may display them rather than on those who have maltreated their race.

Church responses

The churches naturally reacted to the almost unbelievable atrocities of the Holocaust. In 1948, the first assembly of the World Council of Churches addressed this message to its constituent churches:

> We must acknowledge that too often we have failed to manifest Christian love towards our Jewish neighbours, or even a resolute will for common social justice. We have failed to fight with all

our strength the age-old disorder of man which anti-semitism represents. The churches in the past have helped to foster an image of the Jews as the sole enemies of Christ, which has contributed to anti-semitism in the secular world. In many lands virulent anti-semitism still threatens and in other lands the Jews are subjected to many indignities.

We call upon the churches which we represent to denounce anti-semitism, no matter what its origin, as absolutely irreconcilable with the profession and practice of the Christian faith. Anti-semitism is a sin against God and man. Only as we give convincing evidence to our Jewish neighbours that we seek for them the common rights and dignities which God wills for his people can we come to such a meeting with them as would make it possible to share with them the best that God has given us in Christ.

Well said. But the acknowledgment is about failing to honour neighbours, rather than failing down the centuries to honour a whole people. And not a word of apology for past sins of the Christian churches towards the Jews!

The Roman Catholic Church, at the Second Vatican Council in 1965 agreed by an overwhelming majority *A Declaration on the Relationship of the Church to non-Christian Religions*. In dealing with the Jews, it contains the following passage:

The Church repudiates all persecutions against any man. Moreover, mindful of her common patrimony with the Jews and motivated by the Gospel's spiritual love and by no political considerations, she deplores the hatred, persecutions, and displays of anti-semitism directed against the Jews at any time and from any source.

Once again, well said; but not a word of acknowledgment or apology for past sins of the Roman Catholic Church towards the Jews! 'From any source' might include the Roman Church; but then again it might not. Nazi persecution took place in Europe, and Europe is predominantly Roman Catholic. During the Nazi persecution the Roman Catholic Church made no open protest to or condemnation of these damnable Nazi policies.

Archbishop Lord Runcie, speaking on the fiftieth anniversary of Kristallnacht in 1988, approached closer to apology:

> The travesty of Kristallnacht and all that followed is that so much was perpetrated in Christ's name. To glorify the Third Reich, the Christian faith was betrayed. The slaughter of the Jews was the desecration of the ministry of Jesus, himself a Jew. Neither inside nor outside Germany did the churches recognise this. And even today there are many Christians who fail to see it as self-evident.

Nothing less than outright acknowledgment and apology from the whole Church is required.

Alone among the Churches which have confessed their guilt towards the Jews is the Evangelical Church in Germany. The Synod of the Evangelical Church there in 1950 published a 'Statement on the Jewish Question' which is often referred to as 'Statement of Guilt regarding Israel'. In it is the sentence:

> We state that by omission and silence we became implicated before the God of mercy in the outrage which has been perpetrated against the Jews by the people of our nation . . . We ask all Christians to dissociate themselves from all antisemitism and earnestly to resist it, wherever it stirs again, and to encounter Jews and Jewish Christians in a brotherly spirit. We ask the Christian congregations to protect Jewish graveyards within their areas if they are unprotected.

The Synod of the Evangelical Church in the Rhineland in 1980 was more terse and direct: 'We confess with dismay the co-responsibility and guilt of German Christendom for the Holocaust.' Excellent as these statements are, they only refer to the Holocaust, not the the centuries of maltreatment by Christians of Jews.

It is almost incredible to me that the Christian Churches

everywhere have not made an open confession and a heartfelt apology for all the evils that they have perpetrated against the Jews century after century after century. As I look back over my ministry in the Church of England of over forty-five years, I feel penitent that I have not done more to try to bring this about. As a Jew I am horrified that those who profess to believe in the God of love should have behaved in such damnable and degrading ways towards members of the race to which Jesus belonged, *and without apology*. As a Christian I am disgusted that the Church of God has not opened its heart in shame and penitence to the Jewish people for the ways in which it has treated them down the years.

The Roman Catholic Church (including the English Church), the Orthodox Churches, the Lutheran Church and the Evangelical Church have all been guilty of discrimination (or at least of tolerating discrimination) against the Jews. It is perhaps particularly surprising that the present Pope (as yet) has not officially apologised for all that his church has done. For he has actually appeared in a Jewish synagogue. A moving pamphlet has described Karol Wojtyla's friendship as a boy with a Jewish boy, Jerzy Kluger, in Widowice in Poland, with whom he still keeps in touch; and he knows what that boy and his family have suffered (Svidercoschi, 1994). The Pope's recent admission that Christians have contributed to Jewish persecution is welcome, but quite inadequate as an apology. Welcome too was the Archbishop of Canterbury's renunciation of his customary patronage for the Church's Ministry amongst the Jews.

I realise that we are not responsible for what our forebears have done in the name of Christ. It is a hard enough task to accept responsibility for the evil we have done without adding to this the sins of our predecessors. At the same time we must disown them and apologise for them and ask for the forgiveness of the race which we have so grievously wronged. This can be done, and it has been done by others in the past (Shriver, 1995), and unless and until it is done, no full reconciliation can take between Christians and Jews.

I began this chapter by writing that when I became a Christian I went over to the enemy. How can any man or woman possibly doubt that the Church has been the enemy of the Jewish people once she or he knows the way in which the Christian Church has treated the Jewish people down the ages? Anyone who becomes a Jewish Christian has to bear in his soul a terrible burden of guilt as a member of a church which has not even apologised for what it has done in the past to his own Jewish people. He must bear it in his soul, and pray for forgiveness and reconciliation. I believe that the Church has done incalculable good. It has brought people to God, and it has taught them the way of holiness. It has inspired countless good works for the relief of men and women and children. It is inspired by the Holy Spirit – but not always. It has also a terrible shadow side. It can act in a way which is incredibly evil and totally contrary to the precepts of its Master and Lord. That is precisely what it has done so far as the Jewish people are concerned.

Would not the millennium be an appropriate opportunity for a confession of sins in the past, and an apology for what the Church has done to the Jewish people down the centuries? I would hope that all churches might join with the Pope and the Ecumenical Patriarch in such an expression of sorrow and regret. I realise that my lone plea is unlikely to move the whole Church at large, but perhaps at least the Churches Together in Britain might issue some such statement as this at the beginning of the year 2000:

We, the representatives of the Churches Together in Britain, wish to take this opportunity at the beginning of the Third Millennium of the Christian era to express our deep and genuine sorrow and regret at the treatment by the Church of the Jewish people down the ages, and in so far as we can apologise for the words and actions of our predecessors, we do so, and we repudiate their actions and words. We are especially penitent about the events which preceded the banishing of Jews from this land in 1290, and the lack of full civil rights accorded to Jews since their return to this country under Oliver

Cromwell until lately. We shall do all in our power to put an end to any anti-Semitism if it may on occasion still be found within our church fellowships.

3

Judaism in relation to Christianity

A Jewish Christian is both Jewish and Christian. Is it possible for him to combine the two? Does he stop being a Jew if he becomes a Christian? Does he have to disown his heritage? Has he, as it were, to start all over again? In order to answer these questions, he has to consider the relationship of his Jewish faith to his newfound Christian faith. He is unlikely to be able to do all this straightaway. In my case it has taken me many years to find answers to these questions, and there still remain aspects of which I am not certain. Some hard thinking is needed to provide satisfactory answers, and this involves what is called theology, that is to say, working out one's beliefs about God. Both the Jewish faith and Christianity are, of course, centred on God. In trying to find the answers to these questions, it is best to start at the beginning.

How it Started

Christianity did not begin as a religion of its own. It started as a sect of the Jews in Judaea. It was a movement of Jews for Jews. At first the earliest Christians felt doubts about admitting non-Jews to their number, but they were persuaded by their leaders that this was God's will because the authentic religious experience of Gentile converts could not be denied. The movement spread among the

43

many Jewish communities of the Mediterranean basin, helped by the tireless work of missionaries, pre-eminent among them the apostle St Paul. By the time that Jerusalem has been captured by the Romans in AD 70, and then later destroyed in the second Jewish revolt of AD 135, the Gentile centres of Christianity had become strong. The focus of Christianity moved from Jerusalem to the predominantly Gentile Christian churches in the Diaspora around the Mediterranean. What was the relationship between this new Christian faith and the ancient Jewish religion? This is not a new question; and to answer it we must go right back to the origins of the Christian faith.

Jesus and Jews

An enquiry must start with the person of Jesus himself, and his recorded utterances in the Gospels, in so far as we can distinguish them from additions or alterations made in the course of tradition. It seems hardly necessary to state the fact, although it has been denied in the past, that Jesus was a Jew, brought up in a Jewish milieu. He thought as a Jew, he spoke as a Jew. He shared a Jewish inheritance and Jewish expectations. 'Jesus the teacher cannot be understood without taking into simultaneous account Jesus the man of God, Jesus the holy man of Galilee, Jesus the *Hasid*' (Vermes, 1983). Jesus himself is recorded as saying: 'I am not sent but unto the lost sheep of the house of Israel' (Matt. 15:24). According to the same evangelist, when Jesus sent out his twelve disciples, he said to them: 'Go not into the way of the Gentiles, and into any city of the Samaritans, enter ye not; but go rather to the lost sheep of the house of Israel' (Matt. 10:5f.). To the Samaritan woman whom he met at the well, the Fourth Evangelist records him as saying: 'We know what we worship: for salvation is of the Jews' (John 4:22). It was not just that his mission was to the Jews: his thinking was Jewish. For example, it was focused on the Kingdom of God. That God is King is central to Jewish belief. In common with other Jews of his time, he expected shortly the end of the age (although he did not know the times and seasons of its coming). We naturally tend to think of Jesus as a person of our own culture and of our own age.

Although the spiritual content of his teaching is timeless, he cannot be properly understood outside his context.

Jews thought of God as so holy that they did not even pronounce his name. His glory (or *Shekinah*) could be experienced on earth, but God himself was beyond thought, Yehovah, I am what I am. And so, because he was a Jew, Jesus recoiled in horror at the idea that anyone should think that he was God. When a rich young man called him 'Good master', he is said to have replied in indignation: 'Why callest thou me good? There is none good but one, that is, God' (Mark 10:17f). In the light of later beliefs about his divinity, no one could have made that up: it must be authentic. Although Jesus rejected the idea that he was God, he did however regard himself as God's special agent in history, and he knew himself to have been filled with God's Holy Spirit. He had been sent to do the will of his Heavenly Father, however costly that might be. And although his mission was to the Jewish people, he never refused people in need, even if they were Gentiles (Manson, 1955). When he upset the tables of the moneychangers in the Jewish Temple, he used a quotation from Isaiah to the effect that the Temple should be a place for all people (i.e., the Gentiles should have a place there as well as the Jews); but he conceived his ministry to be oriented towards his fellow-Jews.

It seems that Jesus did not claim to be the Messiah. In the account of his trial before the High Priest in St Matthew's Gospel, when he was asked 'Tell us whether thou be the Christ, the son of the Blessed?' he replied 'Thou sayest'. Although later, after his resurrection, his disciples called him the Messiah (and Christ, the Greek form of the word, became almost his surname), Jesus preferred to describe himself by the enigmatic phrase 'Son of Man'. The Hebrew word 'Messiah' means 'The Anointed One', the one set apart to save Israel. In Jesus's day there was no consensus about what the Messiah would do, but the general expectation was that he would 'restore the kingdom again to Israel' (Acts 1.6). Jesus knew that he was sent to proclaim and to initiate the Kingdom of God rather than to restore Israel's sovereignty, so he never used the word 'Messiah' of himself.

According to the Gospels Jesus was addressed as God's 'beloved son' at his baptism, and this is repeated in the account of his transfiguration on the mountain top; but in his recorded sayings he did not claim the title for himself. In any case the phrase in the Jewish thought of his day did not have the metaphysical connotation that it was later given in Christian tradition. In the Gospel of St Luke, for example, in his account of the angel's words to Mary at the Annunciation, there occur the following: 'And he shall be called the son of the Highest and the Lord God shall give unto him the throne of his father David.' These recall the words of Samuel, speaking to David of the royal house which he was to found: 'I will be his father and he shall be my son' (2 Sam. 7:14). The words denote close filial relationship rather than metaphysical status.

As a Jew it was natural for Jesus to honour the Torah, and to keep the Jewish Law. He did not himself abrogate it; indeed, he is reported as saying 'Think not that I am I come to destroy the law, or the prophets: I am not come to destroy, but to fulfil' (Matt. 5:17). He did not agree with all the contemporary interpretations of the Law, and at times he dissented strongly from these. But he himself kept the Law. The only exception would seem to be when he ordered a disciple to follow him rather than bury his father: 'Let the dead bury the dead' (E.P. Sanders, 1985). At his Last Supper he spoke of his sacrificial death in terms of a new covenant, but there gave no hint that he believed that his coming in any way abrogated the old covenant which God had made with Abraham, or that God had renounced the election of Israel, even though, through their inability to see the things that belonged to their peace, 'their house shall be left desolate'.

Paul and the Jews

Jews sometimes claim that Jesus was simply a Jewish prophet, and Paul was the real founder of Christianity. I do not think that that claim can be substantiated, if only because Paul tells us on oath, in his letter to the Galatians, that he had approval for his gospel from the chief Christian authorities in Jerusalem. Paul also was a Jew, and proud of it too, whatever his fellow Jews may have thought of him. He was a Jew of the Diaspora, born in Tarsus, and conversant with Hellenistic ways of thinking. When writing epistles to Gentile Christians in the Diaspora, Paul used imagery and language common in the Hellenistic world which, if taken literally, would seem to accord with the higher Christology later accorded to Jesus. But according to the author of the Acts of the Apostles, when Paul addressed Jews in Jerusalem he is reported simply to have made no greater claim than this: 'I am a Pharisee, the son of a Pharisee: of the hope and the resurrection of the dead I am called in question' (Acts 23:6). In other words, he was claiming to be a good Jew, and the only point of contention with the Jews concerned his belief in Jesus's resurrection. A little earlier, Paul had been taking a Jewish vow of purification in the Jewish temple (a very Jewish thing to do), and after his presence became known a riot had ensued. These were the accusations which the rioters were said to have made against him: 'This is the man that teacheth all men everywhere against the people, and the law, and this place; and further brought Greeks also into the temple and hath polluted this holy place' (Acts 21:28). In other words, the author of Acts is informing us (and he may have had his own agenda for so doing) that the real grievance that people had against Paul was not about Jesus, but about his alleged negative teaching about the Jewish Law and his relaxed attitude over Gentile Christians whom he had brought into the Temple.

Paul dispensed Gentile Christians from keeping the Law, but as a Jew he kept the Law himself and, according to what he wrote in his Epistle to the Romans, he could not actually bring himself to call it bad: indeed, it was good, even if it did result in condemnation. Again, when writing to the Church in Corinth, he does not deny that the old covenant was glorious, even if its glory was eclipsed by the glory of the new covenant: in other words, the old covenant was still operative. Even the author of the Epistle to the Hebrews, although he describes the new covenant which had been prophesied by Isaiah and inaugurated by Jesus as a 'better covenant', only calls the earlier covenant with Abraham 'old', adding that 'that which decayeth and waxeth old is ready to vanish away' (Heb. 8:13). Even he cannot bring himself to say that it has already been abrogated, and the reference is probably to the imminently expected end of the era when all would be changed.

It is in his letter to the Romans that Paul gives his most systematic account of his Christian thinking, and in chapters 9 to 11 he deals with the Jewish people in relation to the Christian faith. Because this is the only place in the New Testament where this is dealt with, it is worthwhile considering the main thrust of these chapters in some detail. Paul did not disown his fellow-Jews: he called them 'my brethren, my kinsmen after the flesh'. He recalled how God had adopted the Jews as his chosen people, how he had glorified them, how he had entered into a covenant relationship with them, and promised that the descendants of Abraham would be blessed. How could Paul possibly disown them? They were Jesus's forefathers after the flesh, his progenitors. Paul drew a distinction between the true Israel and the rest in a typically Jewish form of argument. Not all the descendants of Abraham constituted the true Israel. The line was traced through Rebecca's younger son Jacob rather than through Esau, his elder brother. This, he declared, may seem to us unfair; but it was God's free and sovereign choice, his 'election'. God saves whom he wills, and who, asked Paul, are we to question his choice? God freely chose Israel to disclose himself, so that it could be a sign to the nations. He did not choose the Jews because they were particularly worthy of his choice. Indeed the story of the Bible shows them often to have been backsliding. The election of the Jews is not due to their own efforts but to God's free choice (and the same principle applies to Gentiles who are called to be Christians), for God would not leave his promise to Abraham unfulfilled.

Paul made no secret of the fact that it was his heart's desire that his 'kinsmen after the flesh' should be saved. He believed that they were not saved. (On this crucial matter I, like many others, strongly dissent.) This was not because they did not believe in God, for he agreed that they actually had 'a zeal for God'. But, according to Paul, the Jews believed that they could obtain salvation by keeping the Law (this was in fact a caricature of Jewish thinking of Paul's time, as scholars now generally agree). For Paul salvation was purely a matter of faith; not just faith in God, but faith in Christ 'who is the end of the law for everyone that believeth'. Christ was their stumbling block. Their non-acceptance of him meant that they were ignorant of God's real righteouness, despite their zeal for God. Faith alone in Christ was what mattered. This, said Paul, applied to Gentiles as much as to Jews. 'There is no difference between the Jew and the Greek: for the same Lord over all is rich unto all that call upon him.' Because the Jewish people as a whole did not have this faith, they were, for Paul, outside the circle of salvation.

Paul went on to ask whether this meant that God has cast off his chosen people. Of course not, he declared. A not dissimilar situation had happened before in Jewish history in the time of Elijah. God had redeemed his promise by saving a remnant who were representative of the whole. He has done it again. So God continues his 'election', and his vocation to the Jews remained, even if the majority were blinded so that they could not accept Christ. This inability of Israel to embrace the promises of God has resulted paradoxically, he claimed, in a great blessing for all mankind. It has brought about the spread of the gospel to the Gentile world. The vast majority of today's Church consists of non-Jews. If the Jews had accepted Christ, Paul implied, this would not be the case; and I suspect that Paul was right there. Christianity would be coterminous with Judaism, and God's blessing to Abraham that all the world would be blessed in him would remain unfulfilled. So God's providence can be seen in the unbelief of the Jewish people.

Paul refused to consider that the present situation in which the mass of the Jewish people refused to accept Christ was the end of the matter. It was, as he saw it, only part of God's plan. God's providence would continue to work itself out. 'Blindness in part has happened to Israel until the fullness of the Gentiles has come in; and so all Israel shall be saved.' Paul, who was a townsman and evidently ignorant of agricultural matters, used the analogy of an olive tree in a somewhat muddled way to illustrate his point. Branches had been torn off (unbelieving Jews) and a wild olive tree (non-Jews) was grafted in. But God is able to graft in again the broken branches (unbelieving Israel) when they have faith. And this will happen when the fullness of the Gentiles has been grafted in. In other words, it was not to be expected that the mass of the Jewish people would embrace Christ until the rest of the world had done so. It was bound to happen in the end, Paul thought, for God cannot break his covenant of salvation with the Jewish people. God cannot go back on his promises. The gifts and calling of God are irrevocable. God has only shut them all up in unbelief so that in the end he may have mercy on all. So far as the gospel was concerned, the Jewish people were the enemies of Christians, Paul declared; but because they were God's chosen people and the inheritors of the promise made to their forefathers, the Jews were the objects of Christian love. Having thus concluded his argument satisfactorily, as he thought, Paul ended with a paean of praise: 'O the depth of the riches both of the wisdom and knowledge of God! How unsearchable are his judgments, and his ways past finding out!'

I have tried here to give an accurate summary of what Paul wrote in these three chapters of his Epistle to the Romans. Although he has some fine insights, I (like many others) find some of his arguments dangerously flawed, as I hope will become apparent in the final chapter of this book.

The widening gap between Jews and Christians

We have already noted the antagonism between Jews and the Christian Church and the way that this was reflected back into the New Testament, especially into St Matthew's and St John's Gospels. There were still Jewish Christians left in Judaea after AD 70 (it is said that they fled to Pella during the siege of the city), but we know nothing about them. It may be that they were the Ebionites, so called because, to the Gentile Church, they seemed to have a 'low' or cheap view of Christ (that is what the word means in Hebrew). They may have still thought of Jesus in Jewish categories: we cannot be sure. At the same time we find in the New Testament the risen and ascended Jesus described at times in ways that imply a more than human status. This is hardly surprising, since 'Jewish monotheism did not at the period involve the utter solitariness often assumed by modern theists' (Houlden, 1992). There had long been a tradition in Jewish piety of 'a second God' whom Philo the Alexandrian Jew at the time of Jesus identified with the Logos or Word of God (Barker, 1992). However this may be, these New Testament descriptions of Jesus contained religious imagery rather than metaphysical definitions of his status. It has been well said: 'Jewish Messiahship does not yield a Christology of status in metaphysical terms of "human" or "divine" origin at all. It yields instead a Christology of function in terms of history' (Dix, 1953). This is not to say that Hellenistic theology was necessarily wrong in defining the person of Christ in metaphysical terms, for it was a necessary attempt to inculturate the Christian faith into categories of contemporary Hellenistic thought. But in so doing the Christian Church inevitably distanced itself further from the Jewish synagogue.

As the Christology of the Gentile Church developed, so its negative view of the Jewish religion hardened. Indeed, in some ways the Church defined itself in opposition to the Jews, for it used the same Scriptures as they did, but interpreted them differently. (It cannot be said that their interpretation was obvious without the presupposition that Jesus was the key to their understanding. Since the Jews refused to accept this, naturally the Church found itself in opposition to them.) For Christians he was the Christ, the Messiah. But as the Jews saw it, Jesus had not carried out the works of the Messiah, who was to appear before the end of the world to usher in a new age; and that age, as they saw it, had not yet appeared. Like others before him, Jesus must therefore have been a bogus Messiah. Not so, said the Christians: he is the Saviour of the world, and the Jews had rejected him. They had had him put to death; they were deicides, murderers of God. For Christians Jesus was divine, the Son of God, the incarnate Word. To the Jews the idea that a man could be God was abhorrent, for this seemed to clash with their basic conviction, as expressed in the *Shema'*: 'The Lord our God, the Lord is one'.

So Christians and Jews grew further and further apart. After the establishment of the Church in the reign of Constantine, the theological gulf was immeasurably exacerbated by the sociological divide as discrimination against Jews grew worse and worse at the hands of Christians. Debates were arranged from time to time between both sides, but neither side reconsidered its position. No serious attempts were made for centuries to see if the gap could be bridged.

Modern reassessments

'All religions are equal'

It is only since the ending of the Second World War, with the consequent disclosure of the full horror of the Shoah, and after the founding of the State of Israel, that a theological reassessment of the relationship of Judaism to the Christian Faith has been attempted. Of course in the eyes of an atheist, Judaism and Christianity are both equal, in so far as they both claim to be ways of relating to a non-existent God. But some Christians and Jews, unwilling to discriminate between the two faiths, take in some ways a similar position. The most facile way to bring about reconciliation is to assert that Judaism and Christianity are equally valid ways of approaching the living God. I do not think that one could say this without at the same time ignoring the obvious differences between all the mainstream religions, including both the Jewish Faith and Christianity. It has been claimed that differences between the various religions' approaches to the unknowable Reality whom we can call God may be accounted for through the differing cultural milieu in which each originated (Hick, 1989).

We should gladly admit that the great religions of the world have much in common, and that Judaism and Christianity have a very great deal in common, since Christianity sprang from Judaism. But some religions are positively evil and repulsive. Bad religion can do terrible harm. In any case, to hold the relativistic view that all religions are equal is to abandon the crucial conviction that it is possible to pursue truth, for it implies that there is no absolute truth and that religions with opposing view can be equally true; and on this account alone it must be rejected. Relativism has a particular attraction for some Jews, because it has never been claimed by them that the Jewish way of life should be imposed upon all, but only upon those who are members of the Jewish people. Relativism is a popular belief at the present time when the contents of other faiths are being studied seriously for the first time, and when people seem to prefer the idea of personal choice to that of objective truth. None the less I find it totally unsatisfactory, because if everything is relative, then anything can be justified; and that is repugnant both to my moral sense and to the pursuit of truth.

'Jesus for the Gentiles, Judaism for the Jews'

Another possible way of relating Judaism to Christianity is to affirm that Judaism is the way to God for Jews, but Jesus Christ is the way, the truth and the life for non-Jews. Although at first sight this would seem a convenient way of disposing of a difficult problem, a little consideration will show that it does not wash. In the first place, what about people like myself who are Jewish, but have become Christian as well? It would seem, according to this way of thinking, that we have gone against the will of God in following Christ; and so it is hardly surprising that I very strongly dissent from such a view. Those who have advocated this solution have simply ignored (as Gentiles so often do) the existence of Jewish Christians. In the second place, it would make a mockery of Jesus as the Great Reconciler who has broken down the middle wall of partition between Jew and Gentile, and has reconciled them by the cross. (The existence of Jewish Christians in a predominantly Gentiles Church is a sign that this reconciliation has actually taken place.) In the third place, it would be absurd to suggest that Jesus, himself a Jew, is the way, the truth and the life for non-Jews, whereas Jews themselves must find another way. Fourth, Jesus never gave any indication that his was the way for Gentiles and not for Jews. On the contrary, he ministered to his own Jewish people, and did not minister to non-Jews unless they specifically came to him for aid. There is not even any indication in Jesus's ministry that he intended his followers to be non-Jews. All of the Twelve whom he chose were Jews. The early Church insisted on its close connection with the Jewish Faith. It was tempted early on to cut itself off from its Jewish origins. Marcion rejected the Old Testament as God's revelation, and believed that it spoke of a different, inferior God to that of the New Testament. While Marcion achieved a considerable following, the Church insisted on holding fast to the Jewish Scriptures, thereby showing both the continuity of the Old and New Testaments and the Jewish origins of the Christian faith. In any case it is hard to credit that God in his providence could have produced two equal ways by which he could be approached by two different sets of people often living in close proximity with each other.

'Judaism is a dead end'

This was the view of most Christians before this century. It was held that because the Jewish people did not accept Jesus Christ they had lost their inheritance and had forfeited the promises of God. Instead of being the chosen people, they had lost the chance of salvation, and the Church instead had taken their place as the people of God. This view, known as 'supersessionism', was very common down the centuries, and it was thought that the loss of the Temple in AD 70 and the loss of their country in AD 135 were concrete signs of the wrath of God upon the Jewish people. Such a view is based on false foundations.

First, the Jews did not put Jesus to death. He was killed by the Romans for political reasons, abetted by the high priests who were appointed by the Romans and who, in their fear that popular feeling in favour of Jesus would bring down Roman wrath upon their heads, deemed it expedient that 'one man should die for the people'. Second, it is clear that the Jewish religion is not a dead end. It is a living and developing faith, and through the practice of their religion Jewish people find themselves in a real and personal relationship with God, whom they serve and love and obey (by keeping the Jewish Law). I can attest this from my own experience. Many Jews show the love that is commanded of them in the Law. Jews can be upright and righteous, caring for their neighbours in ways which can put to shame many Christians. It is wrong to equate Judaism today with the plain text of the Hebrew Scriptures or with any one of the sects of first-century Palestine. The point has been put well in a recent Lambeth Conference report *The Truth Shall Make You Free* (Church House Publishing, 1988):

Its definitive works, such as the Mishnah and the Talmud, as well as its current liturgy, were produced by post-Pharisee Rabbis in the same period, the first to the fifth centuries, within which the Fathers of the Church were defining the meaning of Christianity. Great care should be taken not to misrepresent Judaism by imputing to it, e.g., the literal interpretation of 'an eye for an eye' which was repudiated by the Rabbis, or the denial of life after death. This is also true of the long standing stereotype of Judaism as a religion of works, completely ignoring the deep Jewish sense of the grace of God. Judaism is a living and still developing religion, which has shown spiritual and intellectual vitality throughout the mediaeval and modern periods despite its history of being maligned and persecuted. The Middle Ages saw great philosophers, such as Maimonides, Scriptural commentators such as Rashi, and poets and mystics such as Moses Ibn Ezra, as well as scientists and interpreters of the Law. Our modern world is inconceivable without the contribution of Jewish thinkers from Spinoza to Buber, scientists such as Freud and Einstein, as well as musicians, artists and others who have helped to shape our cultural life; we are, to our loss, less knowledgeable of the creative vitality of spiritual Jewish movements of recent times such as Hasidism and Musar.

'Jesus is the fulfilment of divine revelation to the Jews'

This is the view which I hold myself, and which I have held ever since I became a follower of Jesus. Jesus was not the fulfilment of the Jewish Faith that most people of the time expected, because, as we have already noted, his concept of messiahship was different from the popular view, and he did not use that word of himself. But it seems to me that when God set apart the Jewish people to be his own, so as to reveal himself through them to the world, the culmination of that revelation could only be God's self-disclosure in terms of human personality. No higher self-disclosure to human beings could be made than through a human being, since we, being humans, understand humanity best, and human beings are made in the image of God. So God disclosed himself uniquely in Jesus.

From all that we know of his reported sayings, Jesus understood himself as sent by God for a special and unique mission to the Jewish people, and knew himself to be the fulfilment of the profoundest of its scriptural prophesies. Jesus, like the canonical prophets before him, accused Jews of being false to the vocation which God had given them, but he never saw himself as discontinuous with the Jewish people. A Report of the Faith and Order Commission of the World Council of Churches, produced in 1967, expresses well how Jesus was the fulfilment of Israel's hope (World Council of Churches, 1988):

We believe that in Jesus Christ God's revelation in the Old Testament finds its fulfilment. Through him we see into the very heart of God; in him we see what it really means to say that God is the God of the covenant and loves man to the very end. As he became the man who was the perfect instrument of God's purpose, he took upon himself the vocation of his people. He, as its representative, fulfils Israel's task of obedience. In his resurrection it has become manifest that God's love is stronger than human sin. In him God has forgiven and wiped out sin and in him created his true covenant partner.

While as a Jewish Christian I would wholly endorse this statement, I am aware that it would be denied by the vast majority of Jews who are of course non-Christians. Orthodox Jews reject Jesus as Messiah. Such terrible harm has been done to Jews in his name throughout the centuries that they prefer not to think about him at all. Some progressive Jews on the other hand regard him as one in the long line of Jewish prophets and teachers. But, unlike Christians, they do not see him as transparent to God, so that we may see through him into God's nature and essence. They do not see him as Israel's representative: on the contrary he has been the unwitting cause of terrible harm to the people to whom he belonged. They cannot see him as the perfect instrument of God's purpose, for he did not, as they understand it, fulfil the role of the Messiah coming at the end of the days to bring in God's Kingdom. They believe that stories of Christ's resurrection arose within the Church and are not based on historical fact. They cannot believe that Jesus was the mediator of the new covenant prophesied by Jeremiah because it has not been their experience at the hand of Christians that in them God has fulfilled his promise 'I will put my law in their inward parts and write it in their hearts' or that as a result of the new covenant 'I will forgive their iniquity and I will remember their sins no more' (Jer. 31:33f.). Jews understand forgiveness of sins as something which God grants to the penitent heart: they do not believe that it has been obtained through the sacrifice of Christ on the cross.

Here then is a major difference between Christians and Jews, in fact *the* major difference. The quotation from Jeremiah cited above describes, as Christians see it, the work of Christ in functional terms. Jews reject this. Put the difference in metaphysical terms and the gulf seems almost unbridgeable, as in the Nicene Creed, when he is defined as 'of one substance with the Father, God of God . . .', who was incarnate through the Virginal Conception of Mary his mother. This is abhorrent to Jews, and the phrase such as 'Mother of God' (as she is described in the orthodox Chalcedonian definition) is to Jews equally objectionable.

Divided opinions among Christians

A covenant is a solemn agreement in which both sides undertake certain promises. God promised to take Israel under his special care, while Israel promised to obey his Law and to keep his commandments. Often Israel failed in its part of the covenant; but God never reneged on it. The promises of God are irrevocable. As we have earlier noted, until recently a contrary view prevailed among Christians, according to which it was almost universally accepted that the new covenant fulfilled in Jesus had superseded the covenant made by God with Abraham. I have earlier considered such a viewpoint, and rejected it. The conclusion I reached that God's covenant with Israel is still valid.

God chose the people of Israel for himself. Israelites were called to serve God, to obey him, and thereby to show him to the nations. True, they disobeyed him on many occasions, and on many occasions they suffered defeat at the hands of their enemies. But a remnant remained faithful, and God made it possible, despite these defeats, to continue the Jews' vocation (as when by the hand of the king of Persia he brought them back from exile). The Jews were under the providence of God, so that his purposes might be fulfilled through him. There are some who believe that, when Jesus the Jew died at the hands of the Romans with the connivance of the High Priest of the Jews, the Jews' election ceased, and passed instead to the Christian Church. But, as we have already quoted from Paul, the promises of God are irrevocable. So often in the Old Testament the Jews were faithless (as Christians are today) but God remained faithful. Of course he still remains faithful. It follows that God still counts the Jews as his chosen people. Why else have they continued down the centuries despite terrible persecutions and disabilities? They still have a destiny to fulfil. He cannot wish them to be assimilated or eliminated. He has a future for them. They remain, in all the vicissitudes of their terrible history of persecution and discrimination, as a standing witness to the faithfulness of God. What other race could have maintained itself and even flourished in the face of such unspeakable treatment? Their very existence, century after century, despite exile and attempted extermination, is a sure sign of God's election, a living proof that God still cares for those who love him but who do not recognise Jesus Christ.

Israel in the Old Testament constituted the people of God, as God's chosen people. Has this inheritance now passed to the Christian Church? Here the point has been so well put by the Faith and Order Commission of the World Council of Churches that I must once more quote from their report:

> Some are convinced that despite the elements of continuity that admittedly exist between present-day Jews and Israel, to speak of the continued election of the Jewish people alongside the Church is inadmissible. It is the Church, they say, that is theologically speaking the continuation of Israel as the people of God, to which now all nations belong. Election and vocation are solely in Christ and are to be grasped in faith. To speak otherwise is to deny that the one people of God, the Church, is the body of Christ which cannot be broken. In Christ it is made manifest that God's love and his promises apply to all . . .
>
> Others among us are of the opinion that it is not enough merely to assert some kind of continuity between the present day Jews – whether religious or not – and ancient Israel, but that they actually are still Israel, i.e. they are still God's elect people. These would stress that after Christ the one people of God is broken asunder, one part being the Church which accepts Christ, the other part Israel outside the Church which rejects him but which even in this rejection remains in a special sense beloved by God.

If the Church and the Jewish people together form the people of God, it follows that there is a close bond between the two, and Christians are in a different relationship to Jews than they are to the adherents of any other faith. I am of strongly of this opinion. 'Jews cannot be treated by Christians as unbelievers but only as brother believers with whom they are privileged to share a common belief in God and the same promises of salvation', states the *Report on*

Christian/Jewish Dialogue of the Overseas Council of The Church of Scotland (Church of Scotland, 1980). This of course does not deny that there are major differences between the two faiths, but they have so very much in common.

Before I was converted to Christianity I knew that I was privileged to be a member of the people of God, and as a Christian I know that I still belong by grace to the people of God. I still worship the same God. If that be regarded as abstract theology, then I can only say that it is validated in my personal experience.

4

Judaism

What does it mean to hold the Jewish Faith? Most Christians imagine that it involves holding the beliefs that are found in the Old Testament, just as most Jews, if asked what it means to be a Christian, would reply that it involves believing that Jesus is the Son of God, otherwise you go to hell. (That is what Jewish undergraduates told me when I was in Cambridge and on one occasion was invited to their Jewish Society.) Both, of course, are wrong.

To hold the Jewish Faith means first of all believing in God, and believing that there is only one God. Hence the *Shema'*, the daily prayer of Jews, taken from the Old Testament: 'Hear O Israel, the Lord your God, the Lord is one.' It also involves believing that God has chosen Israel for his special purposes, to make himself known and to make his will known for all people. His will for the Jews is enshrined in the Torah, the first five books of the Bible, attributed to Moses. Those are the essentials of Jewish belief. But there are many different interpretations of this Faith (just as there are many interpretations of Christian belief). This was the case in New Testament times, as it still is today. Again, it is popularly supposed that the Jews were either Pharisees or Sadducees, because these are the two sects mentioned in the New Testament. In fact there were many sects. Josephus, the Jewish writer who wrote about the Jews after the fall of Jerusalem in AD 70, mentioned four 'ways' (that is, Sadducees, Pharisees, Essenes and what he calls The Fourth

Philosophy). (In fact, he used the word *haireseis* from which our word heresies is derived, but he meant by that just sects or ways of living the Jewish life.) The Jerusalem Talmud also reports that there were no less than twenty four sects of heretics at the time of the destruction of the Temple in AD 70. In addition to these more sophisticated interpretations of Judaism, there was the way of the *'am ha-aretz*, the people of the land, who sat light to many of the details required for Jewish practice. (It is the same today in the Christian Church: there are many Christian 'people of the land' who sit very light indeed to Christian practices.)

Not many Christians realise that Orthodox Jews hold as divinely inspired not merely the Jewish Bible (the contents of which were not finally settled by the Jews until more than half a century after Jesus had been crucified) but also other compilations as well. The first of these is the Mishnah, a book of laws rather than a law book (Cohen, 1992). It contains rules about institutions like the Temple and the Jewish *Sanhedrin* (Council), about religious authorities (like the High Priest), and rituals (such as the sacrifical cult in the Temple, although this no longer existed when it was compiled). It gives opinions of the rabbis from AD 10 to 220, who were known as the *Tannaim*, and does not attempt to adjudicate when they differ. It was completed around AD 220 in Palestine by sages who gathered at Jabneh after the Romans had destroyed Jerusalem in AD 135. In addition to the Mishnah, there is the Talmud, which is really an authoritative commentary on the Mishnah, and which also includes much else, such as legend, folklore and popular religion, containing the views of later Jewish sages, known as the *Amoraim*, up to AD 500. It exists in two editions; the Palestinian being compiled by AD 400 and the Babylonian by AD 500, although they were probably not written down until later. (Babylonia became the focus of Diaspora Judaism, a sort of 'capital' for the Jewish faith after the Christian authorities had made things very difficult for them in Palestine.)

So Orthodox Jewry holds as sacred not only the Scriptures (written Law) but also tradition enshrined in the Mishnah and Talmud (oral Law), in the same kind of way as the Roman Catholic Church regards as of equal authority the Word of God both in the

Scriptures and in the tradition of the Church. In the words of the Second Vatican Council, in its Dogmatic Constitution on Divine Revelation: 'Sacred tradition and sacred scripture form one sacred deposit of the word of God, which is committed to the Church.' Although of course the content of revelation as understood by Orthodox Jews and Roman Catholics is very different, their holding together of Scripture and tradition is surprisingly similar.

Not all Jews have held tradition sacred in this way. There arose a sect in Persia in the ninth century which rejected the Talmud and held only the Jewish Scriptures to be divinely inspired. This sect, known as the Karaites (people of Scripture) has lasted over a thousand years, and earlier this century there were said to be over ten thousand adherents in Russia. There are even a few in Israel. At one time there was a significant Karaite literature in philosophy, theology and scriptural exegesis, and the sect spread among Jews into many parts of the Diaspora. Its adherents believed in an individual rather than an authoritarian interpretation of Scripture. There is a remarkable parellel here with the Christian Reformation, with its catchword *sola Scriptura* (solely by Scripture) and with Luther's claim for the private interpretation of Scripture. Once again, the content of Scripture is different, the Karaites of course being concerned only with the Hebrew Scriptures, while the Reformation was concerned with the Bible of both Old and New Testaments.

The Orthodox Church separated from the Catholic Church in the West in 1054, and although there were important points of belief in common involving in particular the authority of the Roman Pope, there was also a divergence of ethos between the Church in Western and Eastern Europe. Here we have two parellel traditions of Christian orthodoxy, basically agreed on the essentials of traditional Christianity, but breathing a very different culture, and not getting on very well together. I have heard the Orthodox Churches compared to a rather aristocratic branch of an ancient family which regards the Catholic Church as a younger brother who is a good entrepreneur and who has made good in business; while the Catholic Church by contrast looks on the Orthodox

Churches as out of date and rather effete in their reverence for their unchanging customs and traditions (and the Reformed Churches as junior and more lowly relations). No doubt this is a caricature; but sociological differences between the churches do exist. In a not wholly dissimilar way there have been sociological differences, in England at any rate, between the two branches of Jewry mentioned in the first chapter, Sephardim and Ashkenazim. The Sephardim in England originated in Spain where, under the Moors, they attained eminence in many professions and were well established in Britain some centuries ago, while the Ashkenazim, generally speaking, have entered the country recently after having to leave their homes abroad where they had been disadvantaged or persecuted, and they have made their way in Britain by their hard work and entrepeneurial talents. I am not suggesting that the correspondences are in any way exact, but I think that it is worth drawing attention to them, since neither Christians nor Jews are likely to be familiar with such a parallel.

Creeds have never played an important part in Judaism, as they have in Christianity. Apart from the *Shema'*, they are never used in Jewish liturgy as they are in Christian worship. On the whole, Orthodox Judaism is more concerned with orthopraxy (doing the right thing) rather than orthodoxy (believing the right thing). I suppose that the nearest thing to a creed in Judaism is the Thirteen Principles of Moses Maimonides. Maimonides was born in 1135 in Cordova in Spain, and was active in Morocco and Egypt. He was a physician, merchant, lawyer and doctor. (He followed the tradition of rabbis in the first century who were always employed in a secular trade.) Since his Thirteen Principles of Faith are not likely to be known to Christian readers, I reproduce them here. I notice that they are included in my (orthodox) Sephardi prayer book, which is odd as they are never used in worship. Here they are:

1.   I believe and affirm that the Creator created and guides all creatures, and that he alone has accomplished, accomplishes and will accomplish all works.

2.   I believe and affirm that the Creator is one, with a oneness

that is absolutely unique, and that he alone was, is and will be our God.

3. I believe and affirm that the Creator is not a body, that there is nothing bodily about him, and that there is none like him.

4. I believe and affirm that the Creator is the first and will be the last.

5. I believe and affirm that the Creator alone is worthy of worship and that we should not worship anything other than him.

6. I believe and affirm that all the words of the prophets are true.

7. I believe and affirm that the prophecy of our teacher Moses is true and that he is the father of all prophets, both of those who came before him and those who followed after him.

8. I believe and affirm that the Torah which is in our possession today is the same Torah as was handed down to our teacher Moses.

9. I believe and affirm that this Torah will not be abrogated, nor shall another Torah come from God.

10. I believe and affirm that the Creator has knowledge of all the deeds and thoughts of men, for Scripture says 'He who has formed their hearts also understands their doings'.

11. I believe and affirm that the Creator rewards all who obey his commandments and punishes those who transgress his prohibitions.

12. I believe and affirm that the Messiah will come. Even should he tarry, I still long for his advent.

13. I believe and affirm that a resurrection of the dead will take place at a time which will be well pleasing to the Creator.

These are still the beliefs of orthodox Jewry today. But not all Jews would phrase their beliefs in this way. Just as Christianity has its reformed Christians, liberal Christians and radicals, so also has

On Being a Jewish Christian

Judaism. Christians are often rightly accused of having been unnecessarily schismatic in the past, and with increasing polarisation they are in danger of becoming schismatic again in the future. Jews of different religious outlooks have also been quarrelsome. For example, the Chief Rabbi (who in fact only represents United Synagogue which comprises some 60 per cent of the Jews in Britain) has been criticised by the Orthodox for attending the Memorial Service (not even the funeral) for Rabbi Hugo Gryn, a greatly loved and respected ex-Auschwitz Jew who belonged to Reform, a more liberal movement within Jewry. This is reminiscent of the excommunication of Lord Mackay, the former Lord Chancellor, by the 'Wee Frees' (a breakaway Scottish Presbyterian Church) for attending the funeral service of a judge who happened to be a Roman Catholic. Religious tolerance is often at a premium in both faiths.

Differences among various Jewish groups primarily concern beliefs about the Torah, and about the authority of the Talmud which lays down rules to be followed in most aspects of life. Reform began early in the last century in Germany, and only reached this country later and in an attenuated form. (In Germany the Reform movement had abolished barmitzvahs, with services held in the vernacular.) The United Synagogue comprises a union of Orthodox synagogues. This used to be a somewhat 'broad church', including people who sat a little light to Orthodox belief and practice, or who were very irregular attenders at synagogue; it has been described as 'Modern Orthodox'. Not all Orthodox Jews belong to the United Synagogue. Some such as the Union of Orthodox Hebrew Congregations, largely formed from the many strict Orthodox refugees who came into Britain from Germany and Eastern Europe, regard them as too lax. There has also grown up the Orthodox Federation of Hebrew Orthodox Congregations based on immigrants from Russia and Poland at the turn of the century. These comprise small congregations in very modest buildings after the model of Eastern European Jews, not wholly unlike the house churches which have lately sprung up among orthodox evangelicals in Britain. Attached to this group are the

Hasidic synagogues, including the Lubavitch. Hasidim are pietistic and intensely religious Jews. The Lubavitch centred around a particular rabbi (called the Rebbe) who acted as their guru, and many of them thought him to be the Messiah.

There was the famous case of Dr Louis Jacob, rabbi of one of the prominent United synagogues in London, the most distinguished rabbinist in Britain and thought to be next in line for the post of Chief Rabbi. However, he wrote a book in which he voiced his opinion that the first five books of the Bible could not have been given by God to Moses on Mount Sinai as they now stand. This produced a furore, and the Chief Rabbi of the time refused to reappoint him as rabbi to his synagogue, nor was he appointed Principal of Jews' College as had been expected. From this there has grown the Masorti movement. Its rabbis are taught at college about modern criticism of the Bible. Although the worship of these groups is traditional in form, the beliefs of their members are not accounted strictly orthodox in content; and naturally there is considerable growth in the movement, especially among young people. Masorti is essentially conservative. None the less the present Chief Rabbi, Dr Jonathan Sacks, has condemned it in very strong terms because it sits light to divine authorship of the Pentateuch: 'An individual who does not believe in *Torah min hashamayim* (the Law from heaven) has cut himself off from *shamayim* (heaven). He has severed his links with the faith of his ancestors.'

The first Reformed synagogue was formed from both Sephardi and Ashkenazi families in 1840. I am surprised that Rabbi Neuberger writes that members of my family supported the split, because in fact Sir Moses Montefiore was then chairman of the Jewish Board of Deputies, and it was largely through his conservative influence that the split came about. Reform had a sincere intention to make Judaism more credible and intelligible to young people. Much of its liturgy is in the vernacular. It is not so radical as Reform in Germany and the United States of America, but its tolerance can be considerable. I have actually been invited to speak at one Reform synagogue in London, but then its Rabbi is a very remarkable man! It is however essentially a reformed orthodoxy, rather than a radical reappraisal. To use a somewhat misleading analogy which might well be objectionable to any Jew who reads this, it is liberal Catholic rather than liberal Protestant. It has made some attempts to redress the very male dominance in orthodox Jewry. Its very first sermon, way back in 1840, stressed the need for parents to be as concerned with their daughters' education as much as their sons'.

Although joined to Reform in the Union of Progressive Jews, Liberal Jews have a somewhat different ethos. Here again I must stick my neck out, because the Liberal movement in Britain was begun by Lily Montague and Claude Montefiore. Claude was a great scholar and benefactor, a very remarkable man. I remember reading his obituary in the library when I was at school, and wishing that I had met him. But he was regarded as far too liberal for my branch of the Montefiore family, which belonged to the orthodox Sephardi synagogue, even if we sat lightly to rabbinic injunctions over food and much else. Claude actually wrote commentaries on the Synoptic Gospels, and when I was earning my living teaching the New Testament, scholars used to ask me whether Claude had been a crypto-Christian. I used to reply: No, he was not. He was always straightforward about what he believed, and although he regarded Jesus as a great, perhaps the greatest, of all the prophets, he was not averse on occasion from strongly criticising him, not least for vitriolic remarks about Pharisees (Kessler, 1989); and he certainly did not think of Jesus as in any way divine.

The Liberal Jewish movement tends to be radical and universalistic. It looks not to the Law of Moses so much as to the moral demand for righteousness in the Hebrew prophets. It is concerned with the purity of the human heart rather than with the orthodoxy of a person's belief or the orthopraxy of a Jew in carrying out the commandments of the Law. It rejects not merely the divine origin of the Torah as coming to us straight from God, but also the divine authority of the Mishnah and the Talmud. Another parallel between Liberal Judaism (and Reform) and Protestant Christianity is that the former admit women to the Rabbinate. Girls as well as boys have a 'coming of age service', the old barmitzvah, roughly parallel to the confirmation in the Catholic tradition of Christian churches.

Liberal Jews originally cut the link between the Jewish Faith and the land of Israel, but in 1937, with Nazi persecution and the need for a place of refuge in Israel, they very properly changed their mind, and Liberal Jews now give strong support to the State of Israel. Unlike their more traditional brothers and sisters, they no longer pray for the coming of the Messiah, for they do not expect him to come. Some have even questioned the need for the circumcision of a male Jewish boy on the eighth day after birth, which has been the hallmark of Jews down the centuries.

My own upbringing was in a Sephardi synagogue, which was in a sense 'broad church', that is to say, its roots were traditionally orthodox and committed to orthopraxy, but it counted among its members people of very different kinds of practice and beliefs. As for my own family, as I have recounted above, we certainly did not set out to keep all the commandments in the Old Testament, of which there are 248 positive ones, and 365 negative ones. For example, my mother certainly did not partake of a ritual bath at the end of each of her periods!

As for the food taboos, as I have said, we only ate fish with fins and scales (and that, alas, ruled out shellfish). We ate no meat from animals that did not have a cloven hoof or chew the cud. I can't remember who our butcher was, but I am fairly certain he did not sell kosher meat – and my father was President of the congregation! (He kept pigs on the land around his holiday house – but he said that was all right as we never ate pork: I believe the same used to happen in Israel.) We had an imaginative cook who, because she could not serve us eggs and bacon for breakfast, devised an alternative which looked (but did not quite taste) just the same; fried eggs on slices of fried salt beef.

We had no qualms whatsoever about taking milk with our coffee after dinner, whether or not we had eaten meat. There is a text in the Scriptures: 'Thou shalt not seethe a kid in its mother's milk.' How can one be absolutely certain, asked the rabbis, whether or not the milk one was drinking did not come from a cow whose calf one had just eaten? The odds might seem very small, but there was just a chance that it might be so. Therefore, no milk after lunch in your sweet or your coffee, and you could only drink it half an hour before you had your lunch. This seemed to my parents rather far gone, and we didn't bother. The rabbinic reasoning here is typical of their desire to put a fence round the commandments, and to produce enactments which would ensure that you kept them whatever your circumstances might be. I suppose that the moral principle at stake is not altogether different from the Catholic casuistical principle of 'tutiorism' that the safer solution is the one that ought to be followed, although I don't think that it was ever taken to the lengths that the Jewish rabbis took it. While all these strict rules undoubtedly served to keep Jewry together when they were a persecuted minority, it was easy to lose the spirit of the Faith in their meticulous observance. But it must be said that to a devout Jew there was much pleasure in keeping to them all, however difficult this might make life, because he or she would know that in this way they were keeping God's laws, and this would make them very glad.

One of the prime commandments in the Torah is to keep the Sabbath holy, and to do no work on the Sabbath. We kept this in the sense that my father, who used to bring back work from the office, never looked at it on Saturdays, although he might on Sundays. I never did homework on a Saturday when I was young. But the rabbis, in their scrupulosity, pronounced that opening the oven door was work, as was pressing the button on a lift or answering the telephone, while of course, driving a car was out of the question. Well, it wasn't out of the question for us. We used to drive to synagogue. In any case our synagogue was more than a Sabbath day's journey from our house, so strictly speaking we ought not to have gone there at all! It is hardly surprising that many Jews felt that the strict observance of regulations was destroying the heart of Judaism, and hence the arrival of liberal forms of the Jewish religion. I suspect too that there was an element of assimilation to British culture here too. Many Jews were determined to be as British as they were Jewish, and therefore there was a tendency to conform as far as possible to British norms, without deserting the essentials of Judaism.

Legal fictions could be devised by the Orthodox to get round some aspects of the law. Thus, it is possible to create an *eruv*, an enclosed area corresponding, as it were, to a domestic backyard which is exempt from the rules about a Sabbath day's journey. This is done by erecting posts which have to be linked up by wire. This is then regarded as a domestic area, and when the suggestion was made that this be done to a chunk of North London, not unnaturally an unholy row broke out! Before we laugh these things out of court, Christians should remember that, if they were brought up in a Catholic tradition, they too had very strict rules to keep. My wife could remember how as a girl she was not even allowed to clean her teeth (lest she swallowed some water) before going to a service of Holy Communion, and there is certainly nothing in the Scriptures about this, just as there is nothing about meticulous Sabbath observance which Victorian Christian families used to enforce on Sundays. Many people can remember being brought up in such a way that no games were allowed on Sundays, no novels, nothing in fact that was fun. Legalism of this kind can infect all religions.

There is an increasing amount of 'mixed marriages' between Jews and Christians, and this has understandably been causing the Chief Rabbi much concern. The practice is going to continue, as we live in an 'open society'. Strangely enough, it was much easier to live as a Jew in the ghetto than in today's society! According to the latest survey, no less than 44 per cent of all British Jews are marrying out of the Faith. Mixed marriages cause great grief all round. Undergraduates used to come to ask my advice from time to time in Cambridge, when a Jew fell in love with a Christian, because it was known that I was a Jewish Christian and they thought that I might help. I used to tell them that they ought to consider before they decided to get married how their children were to be brought up: as Jews or Christians or (if this is possible) a bit of both? ('Mixed marriages' so often result in a family ceasing to practise any religion at all.) If they decided that they would go ahead and get married, I used to beseech them to do this in a way that, if at all possible, did not alienate their families. Some Jewish parents go into mourning in such cases, and they have even been known to bid farewell to their children for ever. It was a pain to me personally when I 'married out' to know that I would be hurting my parents. My father, who really did love my bride and had been very kind of her, none the less wept throughout our wedding! It is particularly painful for parents when their son marries a Gentile, because according to Jewish Law Jewish inheritance passes not through the male but through the female – heaven knows why – and so their grandchildren cannot be regarded as Jewish. (This does not apply to Liberal and Progressive Judaism in England.) Christian parents can be deeply upset by mixed marriages too. It is not worth having a church or synagogue public ceremony if the result will be family disruption. Better have a private ceremony, and a public reception; or even a registry office ceremony with some prayers at the reception. At least, that is what I used to advise.

Of course, the matter could be resolved by one of the couple becoming a Christian or a Jew. I personally would never consent to baptise a person and prepare someone for confirmation on these grounds, unless I was clear that conversion was a matter of faith on the part of the person concerned, and that no pressure had been put upon her. In my family it has on occasion happened the other way round: the fiancé became a Jew. However, it is not all that easy for non-Jews to become Jewish. Anyone might think that Jews did not want Gentiles to join the chosen people! This is odd because way back in New Testament times Judaism was a proselytising religion with large numbers of converts in the Hellenistic world. Not so today! Even Liberal Judaism requires a year or more study, some knowledge of Hebrew and an interview before a board. Orthodox Jewry requires much more, including living for a time in an Orthodox family. And of course there is the ritual bath before admission, and circumcision for all males, a painful event for an adult. I would have thought that a religion that is bewailing the loss of so many of its members through assimilation and mixed marriages would be well advised to consider being more open in receiving converts than it seems to be at present; but that is their affair.

In writing about Judaism I have been concerned with it as a religious institution, and I have noted some parallels between Judaism and Christianity. I have pointed out the difficulties that occur when the two Faiths intermingle in marriage. More fundamental however is the question whether the two Faiths could ever come together again. After all, there was a time, at the very beginning of the Church, when the disciples were happy to worship in the Jewish Temple in Jerusalem, and we must imagine that they worshipped in Jewish synagogues until they were *aposunagogoi*, cast out of the synagogue, about which we read in later New Testament writings. Here I have to say that I have no difficulty in worshipping from time to time in a Jewish synagogue. To take a recent example, at my brother's memorial service, and later, before the setting of his tombstone, evening service according to the Jewish Sephardi rite was said and sung in Synagogue. (In Bevis Marks for the Memorial Service, ladies sat downstairs with the men; but in the Ramsgate synagogue the ladies, to their great chagrin, were banished to the gallery.) I found that I was very happy to join in (although my Hebrew was a bit rusty, and from time to time I got lost). There was nothing in the prayers with which I wished to disagree, and that is also the case when I am present at a Seder Night service on Passover Eve, although of course I inwardly dissent whenever there is a prayer that the Messiah shall come 'speedily in our days'.

I shall be examining in the next chapter the differences between Christianity and Judaism, and I shall consider whether there is not any possibility of them being bridged. There is however one area where Christians and Jews have already met, and indeed members of other faiths as well. I refer to mystics, Jewish mystics and Christian mystics.

Attempts to limit mystical truth – the direct apprehension of the Divine Substance – to the formulae of any religion are as futile as the attempt to identify a precious metal with the die which converts it into current coin. The dies which the mystics have used are many. Their peculiarities and excrescences are always interesting and highly significant. Some give a sharper, more coherent impression than others. But the gold from which this diverse coinage is struck is always the same precious metal: always the same Beatific Vision of a Goodness, Truth and Beauty which is *one*. (Underhill, 1923)

The history of mysticism in the Christian tradition is comparatively well known, but Jewish mysticism remains to many people somewhat obscure. There have been individual mystics like Moses ben Ezra; but the Jewish tradition is mostly bound up with Kabbalistic thought.

According to the most recent research into the Kabbala by Moshe Idel, from the beginning of Jewish mysticism in the second century BCE there were two types of mystical experience, though from the start they cannot be clearly distinguished . . . The first was the moderate form, which led the mystic through dedicated study of the Torah to the mysteries of the eternal pre-existent Torah and thus to contemplate, indeed to influence, the Godhead itself. The second was the intensive form, which aimed at the ecstatic fulfilment of the mystic through particular techniques (magic words, the singing of divine names and hymns). (Küng, 1992)

Kabbala means literally tradition, but it came to be used of the secret teaching of Jewish tradition, gnostic in its direction, which flourished in the Middle Ages and which became less secret with the publication of tractates and writings. Early Kabbalistic writing is summed up in the thirteenth-century Book of Zohar. Kabbalistic thought is about our pilgrimage to the Being of God through emanations and angels. The divine chariot of Ezekiel provided imagery through which mystical thought could express itself.

The Habitations of the Spiritual Castle through which St Theresa conducts the ardent disciple to that hidden chamber which is the sanctuary of the living God . . . the mystical paths of the Kabalistic tree of life, which lead from the material world of

Malkuth through the universes of action and thought, by Mercy, Truth, Justice and Beauty to the Supernal Crown; all these are different ways of seeing this same pilgrimage. (Underhill, 1911)

Kabbala, popular as it was in Jewish spirituality, remained peripheral to Jewish thought, and was subject to disapproval by many rabbis, for Judaism, like Christianity, is basically a prophetic rather than a mystical religion, in which God discloses himself in the realm of history rather than through ascending from this world into mystical spheres of being. In Eastern Europe it fused with the Ashkenazi movement of Hasidim (meaning 'The Pious Ones') which combined intense religious experience with deep religious piety.

However, it is not through mysticism, but through the Scriptures, that Judaism and Christianity have the most common links. The Christian doctrine of creation, the Christian doctrine of humankind, the Christian doctrine of the Fall, are all derived from the Jewish Scriptures, although the Jewish doctrines differ in some respects from the Christian ones. The transcendence of God is a fundamental Jewish belief which Christians inherited. The immanence of God, developed in the Jewish doctrine of the *shekinah* and the Christian doctrine of the Holy Spirit, both find their basis in the Jewish Scriptures. The canonical prophets in the Old Testament, that is to say, Isaiah, Jeremiah, Ezekiel, Amos, Hosea and others, have had a formative impact on Christianity, and of course these come from the Jewish Scriptures, and form a vital part of Jewish religion. The Psalms, which are recited daily in Anglican and Roman Catholic offices, and which have had a vast influence on Christian spirituality: these are the psalms of David, which form a large part of Jewish liturgy as well as Christian public worship. After all, Christianity like Islam is an offshoot of Judaism, and there is a great deal in common between all three Faiths. It is this common origin, and the common basis of Judaism and Christianity, which makes the rupture between the two Faiths so tragic. But however much they have in common (and it is a great deal), nothing can obliterate the great gulf between them over Jesus Christ, who after all forms the central focus of the Christian religion.

5

Jewish and Christian differences

Although Christianity began as a sect within Jewry, real differences of belief have developed between what must now be called the two distinct Faiths. There is, as we have seen, a very great deal of agreement. As Pope John Paul II told a group of Jews in 1982, Christianity and Judaism are 'linked together at the very level of their identity'. I would say that the two Faiths agree far more than they disagree. The following is a summary, by no means exhaustive, of the basic elements of Judaism which has been made by a distinguished Liberal Jewish thinker; and to a large extent these are shared by Christianity:

1. The faith of Abraham and of the patriarchs in the God who has chosen Israel with irrevocable love.
2. The vocation to holiness ('Be holy, because I am holy'; Lev. 11:45) and the necessity for conversion (*teshubhah*) of the heart.
3. The veneration of Holy Scripture.
4. The tradition of prayer, both private and public.
5. Obedience to the moral law, expressed in the commandments of Sinai.
6. The witness rendered to God by the 'sanctification of the name' in the midst of the peoples of the world, even to the point of martyrdom if necessary.

7. Respect and responsibility in relation to all creation, committed zeal for peace and for the good of all humanity, without discrimination. (Martini, 1990)

Nonetheless some of the disagreements between the two Faiths are very fundamental. As a Jewish Christian, perhaps I can explain to Christians why Jewish belief has developed as it has, and to Jews why Christians hold the views that I do, although I do not pretend to be able to bring the two sides together.

Baptism

It seems right to start at the beginning, and that means baptism, especially as in most Christian traditions infants are baptised. For Jews, the baptism of a Christian is a crucial moment. It is sad enough for them when a Jew is converted to Christianity, but it is calamitous when a Jew is baptised as a Christian. I think that the reason for this is twofold. In the first place it brings back folk memories of compulsory baptism that so many Jews have had to undergo in past ages at the hands of Christians, and secondly baptism was the means of entry into civilised society (if I may so put it) in Germany after the Enlightenment when so many secularised Jewish families drifted into the Christian Church. These memories hurt, and they are revived today when a Jew is baptised into the Threefold Name as a Christian. (Baptism itself is derived from Judaism, and a ritual bath is still required by the Orthodox before a Gentile is admitted to the Jewish Faith.)

There is, I think, another reason, and that is connected with circumcision. I was circumcised on the eighth day after my birth, and there was therefore imprinted on my body (and in a very personal part of my body) the sign of the covenant which God made with Abraham, and which was to be a continuing sign of the covenant for successive generations of Jews. It is a sign so clear and unmistakeable that circumcision was used both in the Roman Empire and by the Nazis to distinguish Jews from Gentiles. Baptism is not that kind of sign: it is a 'once only' action that cannot be repeated, because it means participation in the one baptism of Christ. None the less baptism is not a subjective feeling, but an outward act, something objective, by which a Christian can be distinguished from others. It does not reflect a passing emotion so much as a continuing commitment. In the case of infant baptism, the parents commit themselves outwardly to bringing up the infant to be a Christian, even if many of them sit light to that commitment. Once someone has been baptised, he or she may later renounce baptismal promises, but the act cannot be undone. That person therefore has 'gone over to the enemy' by means of an unrepeatable act. That is another reason for the Jewish abhorrence of Christian baptism for one born of their own race.

Of course, there are many other theological interpretations of baptism. It is a sign of death and resurrection (at least it used to be, when the baptisand went under the waters of baptism to 'drown' with Christ: the modern method of 'sprinkling' almost completely obscures that meaning). It is a washing away of original sin, whatever precise meaning may be given today to that phrase. It is a sign of regeneration or rebirth, just as our first birth came from the water of the womb. And so on, But these theological interpretations pass most people by. They are meaningful to clergy and to theologians, but not to most ordinary people. For them baptism means predominantly entry into the Christian Church, to be taken on trust at birth in the same way as everything else at birth is taken on trust from one's parents, even if later it may be repudiated.

That is why even the baptism of an infant is such a serious matter in the eyes of Jewry. I am reminded of the Mortara case, which I have mentioned earlier, when a Jewish boy was baptised as a boy by a servant girl, removed forcibly from his parents and brought up as a Christian. Of course such atrocity stories do not take place nowadays; but the event illustrates the importance in which baptism was held both by Christians and by Jews.

In the light of this, it is not hard to see why my baptism at the age of sixteen was a shock to some of my fellow Jews.

Confirmation

The ceremony which is to some extent the equivalent of confirmation in the Christian Church is *barmitzvah* for a Jewish male of the age of thirteen. Some non-Orthodox Jewish congregations also have a service for females at the age of fourteen, and in some forms of progressive Judaism the occasion is actually called 'confirmation'. In the Sephardi tradition, the young boy, when called to the Law, recites this prayer before the blessing:

O my God and the God of my forefathers! On this solemn and sacred day, which marks my passage from boyhood to manhood, I humbly venture to raise my eyes unto thee, and to declare, with sincerity and truth, that henceforth I will obey all thy commandments, and undertake and bear the responsibility of all mine actions towards thee. In my earliest infancy I was brought within thy sacred covenant with Israel, and today I again enter, as an active responsible member, the pale of thine elect congregation, in the midst of which I will never cease to proclaim thy holy name in the face of all nations.

Do thou, O heavenly Father, hearken unto this my humble prayer, and vouchsafe unto me thy gracious blessings, so that my earthly life may be sustained and made happy by thine ineffable mercies. Teach me the way of thy statutes, that I may obey them, and faithfully carry out thine ordinances. Dispose my heart to love thee and to fear thy holy name, and grant me thy support and the strength necessary to avoid the worldly dangers which encompass the path lying before me. Save me from temptation, so that I may with fortitude observe they holy Law, and those precepts on which human happiness and eternal life depend. Thus I will every day of my life trustfully and gladly proclaim: 'Hear O Israel! The Lord is thy God! The Lord is one!'

This prayer may appear rather fulsome when translated into English, but at the same time it seems, at first sight, to be similar in intention, *mutatis mutandis*, to the prayers of a Church of England confirmation. However, in the *barmizvah* prayer there is no mention of the Holy Spirit, whereas confirmation is concerned as much with the confirmation of the Holy Spirit as it is with the confirmation of baptismal promises. The bishop prays that each confirmed may 'daily increase in the Holy Spirit more and more', and according to the Alternative Service Book he prays: 'Confirm your servant with your Holy Spirit'.

Not that Jews disregard the Holy Spirit. On the contrary the sentence in the Anglican Morning and Evening Prayer: 'Take not thy Holy Spirit from us' is actually taken from a Jewish Psalm. At the same time, Jews expect people to get on with things. In Christian parlance they might be said to be semi-Pelagian or almost Pelagian. They do not take such a serious view of sin as we find in the writings of St Paul and which is reflected in our Christian liturgies. According to the Christian view, a person is either dead in his or her sins, or else 'very far gone from original righteousness' (according to the Thirty-Nine Articles), so that spiritual regeneration by the Spirit is needed to be born again as a Christian. It follows that the work of the Holy Spirit is constantly needed in order to prevent relapse into spiritual death. But according to Jewish thought as developed by the rabbis, human beings are born with the *yetzer hara*' (the evil impulse), and at the age of thirteen there appears, with the dawn of moral consciousness, the *yetzer hatob* (the good impulse).

The common opinion was that the evil impulse is just the disposition of the human being which results from natural instincts, especially sexual desire. Consequently it is not something that is essentially bad, since God creates only what is good. It is evil only in so far as it is liable to be misused . . . So the urge, although it eventuates in wrongdoing, is an essential equipment of man and indeed grants him the opportunity of becoming a human being; because without it there is no possibility of his doing evil, and, as a consequence, goodness also would be meaningless. (Cohen, 1932)

Such a view might be received with sympathy by many Christians today. But it is clearly in conflict with the traditional Christian view that spiritual regeneration or rebirth is necessary for eternal life, and that the Holy Spirit is constantly needed to prevent relapse.

The Scriptures

Christian fundamentalists hold that all the Scriptures are verbally inspired, in the same way as Orthodox Jews hold that the Scriptures are inerrant, unalterable and coherent, and that the Five Books of the Law contain the Word of God written by Moses (including the description of the prophet's death!). Reform Jews, without holding such an extreme view, hold that all the Scriptures are inspired, as do Christian evangelicals. Liberal Jews, like liberal churchmen of all traditions, venerate the Scriptures, but believe that they should be read with discrimination. Thus there is apparently a great similarity between Christians and Jews on the subject of the Scriptures.

But there are also some differences. For example, Orthodox and Reformed Jewry regard the Books of Moses as the most important part of the scriptural canon, while Christians (in common with Liberal and Progressive Jews) look primarily to the canonical prophets for inspiration.

The greatest difference of all lies in Christian views about the relationship of the Old to the New Testaments. Neither Christian nor Jewish interpretation of the Hebrew Scriptures was by any means straightforward. Rabbis attempted exegesis, but they might also carry out *eisegesis* (reading ideas not out of but into Scripture). What they did not do and could not do was to understand Scripture as foreshadowing the events of the new covenant inaugurated by Jesus Christ, either directly or by allegory or typology or by any other means; nor could they understand any of its contents as prophecies of Jesus. The Jews certainly looked to their Scriptures for prophecies of the coming Messiah. No less than 456 passages have been identified which are in ancient rabbinic writings applied to the coming Messiah (Edersheim, 1883). Of these, 75 are found in the Pentateuch, 243 are taken from the prophetic writings, and the remaining 138 from the remaining Old Testament books. These ascriptions to the coming Messiah are found in no less than 558 quotations from early rabbinic writings. But none of these were understood as referring to Jesus.

The early Church did not discard the Hebrew Bible. It was useful to them for apologetic; it enabled them to argue with the Jews from an acceptable startpoint. When Marcion, who believed that the Old Testament was about a different God from the Father of our Lord Jesus Christ, rejected the Old Testament and severely curtailed the New Testament, the Church responded by keeping the whole of the Old Testament within the canon of Scripture.

Isaiah 53, with its prophecy of the Suffering Servant, shows up the differences between Jewish and Christian interpretations. Modern scholarship tends to regard all the Servant Songs in Isaiah as referring to Israel. Some scholars, however, have thought that these refer to a pious minority within Israel such as the prophets, while others have held that some historical person, such as Zerubbabel or Jehoichin was intended (Wade, 1929). But these passages can have a *sensus plenior*, a deeper meaning than that of their original context. Christians have regarded them as prophetic of Jesus Christ, even though Jesus in his recorded utterances never himself refers to them. Jewish interpreters have understood the passages very differently. A full study has been made of their various interpretations (Driver and Neubauer, 1876). In the Targum of Jonathan (the biblical paraphrase in Aramaic which probably dated originally from New Testament times) all references to the suffering of the Servant were obliterated. 'He was smitten' in the Hebrew becomes 'though we were accounted smitten' in the Aramaic. By the time of Origen, it is clear from his dialogue with Celsus that Jews then regarded the Servant Songs as referring to the whole Jewish nation. God had promised resurrection to the Jewish people after their many sufferings on behalf of the Gentiles. Many rabbinical interpreters however did understand the passage messianically. Some spoke not of the Messiah's death, but of his closeness to death or his readiness to die. Others could accept a suffering Messiah, but not one who was put to death by such an ignominious death as crucifixion. As Trypho is reported to have said to Justin Martyr, 'The Messiah would die but not by crucifixion'. The Messiah might even have to accept vicarious suffering, but not a propitiatory death. No doubt Jewish exegesis was partly in reaction to that of Christians, but here is a clear distinction between the two sets of interpretations.

Jesus interpreted the Scriptures of himself (Dodd, 1952), somewhat in the same way as the Essenes of the Dead Sea Scrolls interpreted them in terms of their Teacher of Righteousness. The early apostles and evangelists continued this tradition, for it enabled them to argue from the known to the unknown, regarding the inspired words of Scripture as prophesies about Christ. (Since the Old Testament Scriptures are relatively unknown today, this method of argumentation has lost much of its usefulness.) It has been well said that 'the first Christians were not concerned with what the authors of the ancient text had wanted to say. That is something which we moderns ask about. They inferred the meaning of the ancient text from the events brought about by God in which they themselves were involved' (Grollenberg, 1988).

Without prior belief in Jesus as the Christ, this method lacks credibility. A few examples will suffice to show this. It is not evident to a Jew who does not believe in Jesus Christ that he should be understood in terms of the Paschal mystery. Why should he? The story of the deliverance of the Jews from Egypt is for them the story of how God delivered their forebears from slavery in accordance with his promise. Why should they understand it as foreshadowing the deliverance from the slavery of sin which Jesus effected on the cross? Again, the author of the Epistle to the Hebrews proves that Jesus, although divine, is not ashamed to regard his fellow human beings as his brothers (Heb. 11:4). He does this by quoting from the Psalms and from Isaiah. But such a proof entails the belief that Jesus speaks in the Scriptures in the first person singular ('I will proclaim thy name to my brethren . . .'). Why should non-Christian Jews believe that? Or again, Peter in Acts 3 quotes from Psalm 16 to prove the resurrection of Jesus: 'For thou wilt not abandon my soul in Hades, nor let thy Holy One to see corruption.'

Why should those who do not accept Jesus as 'thy Holy One' understand this as a prophecy of the resurrection?

I am not suggesting that Christians are wrong to understand the Hebrew Scriptures in these ways. Indeed, I think that they are right to do so (and I do so myself), given belief in Jesus Christ. I am only concerned to point out that this kind of interpretation is not in itself self-evident. It depends upon a prior belief in Jesus as the Christ. 'Proof texts' cannot be read directly out of the text as it stands. In a sense they are *eisagesis*, a reading into the text of what is known on other grounds to be true. Those who do not believe this find that these 'proof texts' lack cogency. These texts belong, I believe, to what is sometimes called the *sensus plenior* of Scripture. The scriptural writers wrote more than they knew. Christians interpret the Scriptures in terms of their presuppositions; and of course Jews interpret them in terms of theirs. There is bound to be a great difference between the two.

The person of Jesus

Many Jews refuse to contemplate the person of Jesus at all. They will not even name him, let alone assess him. All they know is that he has been a curse to their forebears, because of the way in which his adherents have treated them.

Not so with Liberal and Progressive Jews. They believe generally that the Christian Church as it developed was not the work of Jesus but of his apostle St Paul, despite the fact that Paul, writing on oath, declared that the gospel he preached, although he received it from heaven, had the approval of Peter, James and John in Jerusalem (Gal. 2:9), and in spite of the fact that Paul in preaching this gospel was scrupulous not to impinge on the territory of other evangelists (2 Cor. 10:16). None the less Paul is generally considered by Jews as the founder of Christianity. According to Leo Baeck 'the old theocentric faith of Judaism is superseded by a new Christ-centred faith' (Friedlander, 1973).

Liberal and Progressive Jews do not accept the Church but they are happy to accept Jesus as a Jew, and as one of the greatest – if not the greatest – of Hebrew prophets. For Martin Buber Jesus was 'his great brother' (Buber, 1962). That and no more. Here is a sympathetic appraisal by a Jewish scholar of repute:

> There was a real Jesus, without any doubt. Over the space of months, or perhaps even the space of two or three years, this Jesus of flesh and blood was seen and heard around the countryside of Galilee and in Jerusalem, an uncompromising, single-minded lover of God and his fellow beings, convinced that by means of his example and teaching he could infect them with the same sense of relation with the Father in heaven. And he did so. The magnetism of this real Jesus was such that not only the shame and humiliation of the cross, and not even the collapse of his ministry, could extinguish the faith of the men and women of his company. But it is now a long time since he was thought of. Very many ages have passed since the simple Jewish person of the gospels stepped back and gave way to the rich and majestic figure of the church's Christ. (Vermes, 1983)

And what is the relevance of Jesus for this liberal thinking Jew? The passage continues as follows:

> Yet it occurs to the historian, as he reaches the end of his presentation of the Gospel of Jesus the Jew, that the world may not have heard the last of this holy Galilean. In this so called post-Christian era, when Christ as a divine form seems to ever increasing numbers not to correspond, either to the age's notion of reality, or to the exigencies of the contemporary human predicament, is it not possible that Jesus the healer, teacher and helper may yet be invited to emerge from the shadows of his long exile? And not by Christians alone? If, above all, the lesson on reciprocal, loving and direct relations with the Father in heaven is recalled and found universally valid, may not the sons of God on earth stand a better chance of ensuring that the ideal of human brotherhood becomes something more than a pipe dream?

* * *

This generous appreciation of Jesus the Jew says nothing about his resurrection, and indeed passes it by. For all its generosity, it is very far removed from the Christ of the Christian creeds. Although not all Jews have denied the resurrection of Jesus, it is crucially important for Christians. After all, it was Paul who said that Jesus was 'declared to be the son of God with power, according to the spirit of holiness, by the resurrection of the dead' (Rom. 1:4). Whatever precise meaning may be given here to Paul's use of the phrase 'son of God', here lies a yawning gap between Jews and Christians over the person of Jesus. Jews did however believe that they would be raised from the dead at the Last Day, and Christians, in speaking of Jesus as 'the first fruits of them that sleep', imply that the Last Days were upon us at Jesus's resurrection, and he was the first to be raised. However, nothing that has happened to the Jewish race since then at the hands of Christians is likely to convince them that for them the Last Days have already begun.

Instead of simply quoting the Christian creeds, I shall set alongside the Jewish view that of a scholar from a different tradition who puts equal emphasis on the Jewishness of Jesus:

We cannot even say that Jesus was a uniquely good and great man. I agree with John Knox that the church's memory can guarantee his 'personal and moral stature', but I also agree with him that history will not produce a figure of sufficient moral goodness to satisfy those who have felt their lives to be ennobled and uplifted by him. History in fact has great difficulty with the category 'unique'. Adequate comparative information is never available to permit such judgements as 'uniquely good', 'uniquely compassionate' and the like ... What is unquestionably unique about Jesus is the result of his life and work. They culminated in the resurrection and the foundation of a movement which endured. I have no special explanation or rationalization of the resurrection experiences of the disciples ... We have every reason to think that Jesus prepared them to expect a dramatic event which would establish the kingdom. The death and resurrection required them to adjust their expectation, but did not create a new one out of nothing. That is as far as I can go in looking for an explanation of the one thing which sets Christianity apart from other 'renewal movements'. The disciples were prepared for *something*. *What* they received inspired and empowered them. It is the *what* that is unique. (E.P. Sanders, 1985)

Many Christians would want to say much more than that. But none would want to say less. There is a great gap between the Jewish evaluation of Jesus the Jew and a Christian's attitude to the risen and ascended Christ. Disbelief by Jews in the resurrection of Jesus and belief in it by Christians lies at its heart.

The biggest gap however concerns the divinity of Christ. For Jews the very idea is almost blasphemous. The opening word of the *Shema'*, the most used Jewish prayer, are 'Hear O Israel! The Lord our God, the Lord is one'. For Jews any hint of the divinity of Christ seems to sin against that great proclamation of the unity of God. How can a man possibly be God, they ask? How is it possible for Christianity to claim that it is a monotheistic religion when Christ is worshipped as God? Here Jews join ground with Muslims in repudiating any form of divinity that may be attributed to a human being.

It is not the object of this chapter to argue in favour of Christianity against Judaism, but simply to spell out the differences that exist, and therefore the big jump that has to be made for a Jew to become also a Christian. Nonetheless, it is necessary to state as clearly as possible the orthodox doctrine of the Trinity and of Christ. The doctrine of the Holy Trinity is not that there are three Gods, but that there is only one God, and that he exists eternally in three modes, as Father, Son and Holy Spirit. Some Christians would say (and I find myself among them) that the actual being of God is shrouded in mystery, and we only know that he is one and eternally one and that his nature is love; and so, while we cannot say that he lives eternally in three modes, we can assert that he shows himself in three modes. And so I do not think that there is necessarily an unbridgeable gap there between Jewish beliefs and Christian doctrine properly understood, especially as there was an oscillation between 'The One' and 'The Many' in the early Israelite conception of God (A. Johnson, 1942), and this tradition persisted even in the intertestamental period (Houlden, 1992; Barker, 1992).

When we come to consider the doctrine of Christ, the gap between Christians and Jews seems to become very large indeed. At the same time we must clarify the orthodox Christian doctrine, which is not that Christ is God, as commonly thought, but that he is God incarnate, that is, God embodied in human personality. I personally regret that Christianity has become so very Christo-centric, whereas the role of Jesus himself was always to point towards his heavenly Father. We have to admit, however, that the language of the Nicene Creed is never likely to be acceptable to Orthodox Jewry. The pre-incarnate Son, it is affirmed there, is 'God of God, light of light, very God of very God, begotten not made, of one substance with the Father, by whom all things were made, who for us men and for our salvation came down from heaven . . .' As a Christian I assent to the Nicene Creed, not because I would express my faith in Christ in that way myself today (I have explained what I would say in some detail, see H. Montefiore, 1993), but because I wish to be a loyal member of the Church, and this is the classic definition of its faith in Christ. His person in the Nicene Creed is defined in terms of Hellenistic metaphysics. This is very far from Hebraic ways of expressing religious truth, and these phrases of the Nicene Creed can hardly be read out of the New Testament. They are the result of the Hellenisation of the Christian faith, which happened when its centre of gravity shifted in its earliest days from Jerusalem to the Gentile world of the Mediterranean.

Had Christianity remained as it began, a Jewish sect, its Creed would never have been defined in such terms. I personally am glad that the Church did spread to the Hellenistic world, as without this it would never have become a world religion. On the other hand, I am sad that the classic definition of Christ is in these terms of Hellenistic metaphysics. How would the person of Christ be expressed in Hebraic terms? Of course here I am only speculating, but I would suggest that it might have been something like this, making use of the word *Shekinah* which the Jews used to express the immanent presence of God on earth: In Jesus the Messiah the *Shekinah* abode fully during his lifetime, so that through him we are in the presence of the Divine. Because he perfectly represented his Father in heaven, he is for us the Son of God. In this way God showed us in human form his divine nature. He died a cruel death on the cross, and this suffering was a sacrifice for us, by which we can be drawn close to God. God raised him from the dead to the highest place in heaven as a kind of first fruits of the day when all will be raised, and in so doing he showed that he was well pleased with his Son. (I was interested to find, after writing the first draft of this chapter, that Levertoff had earlier been exploring a similar use of the Hebrew *shekinah* (Gillet, 1939)). If the Christian faith had been expressed in phrases of that kind, I suggest somewhat hesitantly that it might be the case that it could be more acceptable to Jews. However it must be said that I see no prospect whatsoever of the Church changing the words of the Nicene Creed to express the full Christian Faith in a way which is more accessible to Jews, so I am reconciled to the fact that my suggestion will fall on deaf ears, and may even earn me brickbats both from Jews and Christians!

The centrality of the cross

There is little in the Old Testament about self-sacrifice as the way to life. There is plenty about sacrifice, the sacrifice of animals in order to be in communion with God. There are passages which illustrate the spirit of self-sacrifice which is willing to bear the sins of others, as when Moses asks to be blotted out of the book of the living if God will not forgive the people their sins (Exod. 31:32), or when David makes a similar plea to prevent others from suffering (2 Sam. 24:17). But it is only in the Servant Songs of the prophet Isaiah that the idea surfaces that death and self-sacrifice could be the gateway to life and salvation. 'It was our sickness that he bore, and our pains, he carried them, while we regarded him as stricken, smitten of God and afflicted. But he was pierced through our rebellions, crushed through our sins, the chastisement to win our peace was upon him and by his stripes was healing wrought for us.' And a few verses later: 'Yahwe was pleased to justify him, and rescued his soul from trouble, caused him to see light and be satisfied, a posterity that prolonged its life' (Isa. 53:4ff., from the translation by Driver and Neubauer).

Later Jewish thought carried the idea that the death of martyrs could be a kind of vicarious expiation (4 Macc. 17:22). To what extent the Servant Songs in Isaiah influenced Jesus in his lifetime is unknown. They are only once quoted in the New Testament, and that in the context of Jesus's healing ministry. It is interesting that, in the Jewish contemporary paraphrase of Isaiah 52:13–53 (Targum of Jonathan), the passage is interpreted messianically. Yet 'everything that could have relation to the suffering and death of the Messiah is artificially explained away' (Taylor, 1951). Earlier in this chapter we have already noted one example of this. Perhaps this is a reaction to Christian beliefs about Jesus as Messiah. More probably it is because of a radically different view of the function of the Messiah. He ushers in the time of complete blessedness. He subdues the enemies of the Jews, brings all people in subjection to Israel, and rules over all the kings and princes of the world. There is no room here for a suffering Messiah. Indeed we have already noticed that the very concept of a personal Messiah has disappeared from contemporary Liberal Judaism, although it remains in traditional Jewish liturgical forms in which Jews pray that the Messiah 'may come speedily in our days'.

Jesus himself seems to have realised that his messianic role was radically different from that of public expectation, and perhaps for that reason he did not use the word Messiah of himself, preferring it would seem the enigmatic phrase 'Son of Man'. We have already noted that one of the reasons why Orthodox Jewry did not accept Jesus as the expected Messiah is because his role was so different from that they expected, and his death was so ignominious that it ill befits a Messiah, or 'anointed one'. I believe it may be the same today. So here again we find deep differences between Jews and Christians: in the first place Orthodox Jews still expect a Messiah, while Christians believe that he has already come. In the second

On Being a Jewish Christian

place, those Jews who do await a Messiah have a different conception of his function compared to that of Christians. In any case 'in the widest circles of Orthodox Judaism, where the messianic expectation is still cherished, the real object of the expectation today is no longer a personal Messiah but only a state of fulfilled time and of perfect righteousness which is understood and described as messianic' (Rengstorf, 1954).

Jews have always felt the need of atonement, for they celebrate *Yom kippur*, the 'Day of Atonement' by prayer, penitence, fasting and abstinence from work. It has always been a very holy day, the only occasion when the High Priest – alone – entered into the Holy of Holies in the Temple. Two goats were set apart, one for the Lord and the other as a 'scapegoat'. The first was sacrificed, and its blood sprinkled before the mercy seat of the holy of holies, and the High Priest laid his hands on the other goat, confessed the sins of all the people, and then let it go into the wilderness. Of course after the destruction of the Temple, sacrifices could no longer take place. In the course of Morning Service the officiant says:

> Sovereign of the universe! Thou didst command us to offer the daily sacrifice at its appointed time; and that the priests should officiate in their service, and the Levites at their stand, and the Israelites by their delegates. But at present, on account of our sins, the temple is laid waste and the daily sacrifice hath ceased; for we have neither an officiating priest, nor a Levite at his stand, nor an Israelite as delegate. But thou hast said that the prayers of our lips shall be accepted as the offering of bulls. Therefore let it be thy will, O Lord our God and the God of our fathers, that the prayers of our lips may be accounted, accepted, and esteemed before thee, as if we had offered the daily sacrifice at its appointed time, and had been represented by our delegation.

Similarly, the sacrifice on the Day of Atonement has been replaced by confession and prayers.

Christians understand the death of Christ as an act of atonement, that is to say, at-one-ment with God. They believe that Christ's once-for-all death replaced the annual celebration of the Jewish Day of Atonement, and one explanation of the death of Christ, to be found in the Epistle to the Hebrews in the New Testament, is dedicated to proving that this is the case, although it carries less conviction in an age when the Jewish sacrifices have been discontinued.

The Christian doctrine of atonement has never been formally defined, nor could it be, because there is a limit to which we humans can probe into the mysteries of God's actions. It has been variously described under images such as sacrifice, ransom, manumission, and reconciliation; and there have been attempts to explain it in more contemporary language. It is not a matter primarily of the forgiveness of sins, for we are always asking God to forgive us our sins, as we forgive those who sin against us. It is rather that we have become alienated from God, and that we are unable to attain atonement and return to a right relationship with him by our own power, but we need some creative action by God to accomplish this for us, and this took place through the death of Jesus. Here there is a difference between Christian and Jewish attitudes, for Jews believe that, given sufficient depth of repentance and faith, we can return to a right relationship with God without the need of Christ's sacrifice.

Although, as we have seen, at the time when the books about the Maccabees were written, and during the period in which Christ lived, Jews believed in the atoning efficacy of a martyr's death, such a belief is far from the Christian belief in the atonement wrought through Jesus Christ. As my Hebrew prayer book puts it in its preface to the services of the Day of Atonement: 'We are bidden to turn to him, we are taught and encouraged to approach him as the repentant son who, with tears in his eyes, draws near to his father. We are told that no intercessor is required, no mediator between us and our Creator, and above all we are assured beforehand of his forgiveness.'

Christians seldom realise these deep divergences of belief between themselves and Jews. The very concept of death and resurrection lie at the heart of Christianity, while for Jews the idea of a Messiah being put to an ignominious death, and of being then raised from the dead, are quite unacceptable. Christians believe that this pattern of life through death is not merely to be seen in Jesus Christ but is repeated in the lives of Christians: indeed it gives us the deepest insight into the secret of life. St Paul gave expression to this when he wrote to the Colossians: 'It is now my happiness to suffer for you. This is my way of helping to complete, in my poor human flesh, the full tale of Christ's afflictions still to be endured, for the sake of his body which is the church' (Col. 1:24 NEB).

This pattern of life through death is to be seen in the lives of Christians, and it is also to be seen in the life of the Church itself. Church revivals have followed periods of deadness in the Church. The Oxford Movement and before that the evangelical revival in Britain give good examples of this. The theme of life through death dominates the two dominical sacraments of baptism and Eucharist. It is not an optional extra but lies at the very heart of the Christian Faith.

The Holocaust

The attempted genocide of Jewry by the Nazis has shaken the civilised world, but it has also left an indelible mark on Jewry as a whole, which Christians can hardly appreciate. There have of course been other genocides in the history of mankind, and even today we have been shown on our television screens the appalling sight of mass killings, measured in hundreds of thousands, in Africa. But it was the cold-blooded planning of the Nazis and the scale and efficient administration of their mass slaughter, using modern technology, that has been so hateful and repulsive that no words can describe it. Jews have been used to violence and repression throughout their long history. Usually this has had a religious cause. But although the anti-Semitism that the Nazis showed had its origins in earlier Christian anti-Judaism, it was a secular version of racial hatred rather than a religious kind of oppression. Although the Church may be accused of being silent and slow to help in this Jewish catastrophe, the Shoah cannot itself be blamed upon Christians.

The Shoah does, however, pose terrible questions for Jews about divine providence. In the past it has been customary for them to account for their persecution by the visitation of divine wrath on their disobedience of divine Law. But this cannot apply to an attempted genocide, which applied indiscriminately to all with Jewish blood. How then could God have allowed it to happen? Are not the Jews his chosen people – how can he allow his elect to be treated in such a terrible way? Jews have found it difficult to give any adequate answer. Some have been forced to give up their belief in God (Rubinstein, 1966). Others have fallen back upon the explanation that God grants humans freedom to sin, although this does not of course exonerate God from all responsibility (Berkovits, 1973). Perhaps God is not omnipotent: God did not will Auschwitz, he wept over it (Lelyweld, 1968). Even to pose the question has been agonising. 'The Shoah is a challenge to all belief in God' (Braybrooke, 1990). To suggest that God is not loving is to deny the whole of the earlier history of his self-disclosure in the Old Testament. To put forward the concept of a suffering God does not really give an answer (Maccoby, 1992). Elie Wiesel in his despair accuses God of indifference. It has even been suggested that there was a 'divine interruption', God interrupting his providence for a time, almost as though his attention was elsewhere (Fiorenza and Tracey, 1984).

Here I would like to make a personal suggestion. Could it be that the pattern of life through death, which the Messiah reluctantly accepted at his Father's hands, makes sense of the Shoah, which is otherwise inexplicable? If it is true that life through death gives us the deepest insight into spiritual reality, and if this is what Jesus himself had to undergo, is it altogether inconceivable that this same pattern of life through death is ordained not merely for the Messiah, but also for God's chosen people? I am interested to note that another Jewish Christian writer has made a similar suggestion (Marcus, 1997). It is perhaps no accident that a contemporary Jewish rabbi has entitled his book on twenty centuries of anti-Semitism *The Crucified Jew* (Cohn-Sherbok, 1992). The very title suggests that what happened to Jesus has been also the fate of the Jewish people. I realise that I am not the first person to make this suggestion. 'In some respects the Jews seem to fulfil involuntarily the mission which the Church tries to carry out voluntarily. They are manifestly the Suffering Servant, the Cross-bearers, although they cannot help themselves and have no choice' (Smith, 1954).

For Christians to suggest that Jews are fulfilling the role of Suffering Servant in no way means that 'they array themselves at the head of the ranks of those who would like to repeat the Holocaust' (Eckardt, 1990). If this fate has come upon the Jews, it is because they are the chosen people of God: it has not been willed in any way by them, nor have they been conscious of the reasons why they have suffered so terribly down the ages and in particular at the hands of the Nazis. Such a concept in no ways reduces the appalling evil of the Nazi regime. The Shoah becomes the latest and most terrible instance of their suffering. If Jesus was indeed the Jewish Messiah, it is not (as has been alleged) 'a profound offence against the sanctity of the unique suffering of Holy Israel' to set one man's death alongside the deaths of six million Jews, especially if chapter 53 of Isaiah can be interpreted as referring *both* to the Messiah *and* to the Jewish people (and, as we have seen, Jewish interpreters have in the past interpreted it in either way). It has been said that 'when it (Christianity) presses Judaism into its own construct, denying Jewish integrity and identity, and when it utilises and misuses Auschwitz in a celebration of Christian triumphalism and supersessionalism, we take issue with Christianity' (Friedlander, 1984). I hope that I am not doing this. I am merely trying to say what, as a Jewish Christian, is the only way in which I can make any sense out of an event so utterly frightful as the Shoah.

I am not saying that the end justifies the means: God forbid! But it is a matter of fact that for the Jewish people new life has come from these terrible experiences of the past. They have emerged from these persecutions, sufferings and murders, with what seems renewed vitality. Is it mere coincidence that post-Enlightenment Jews, out of all proportion to their numbers, have today become leaders in so many fields of life; industry, commerce, medicine, philosophy, sociology, art, music, politics and so on? Persecution, far from blotting them out, seems to have given them new energy and inner resources. Prejudice, far from keeping them down, has been the springboard from which in so many fields they have risen to the top, often by so doing incurring envy on the part of their Gentile neighbours.

Forgiveness

There is a difference between Jewish and Christian views about forgiveness, a subject which naturally follows on from a consideration of the Holocaust. According to the Jewish view, before a person can be forgiven there must first be repentance. Sins must be acknowledged and confessed, and, after fasting and confession, the penitent must show by acts of restitution and by a changed character that the repentance is genuine. It follows therefore that God alone can forgive those who perpetrated the Holocaust. And so Jews today, including those who escaped from genocide, may justifiably feel bitter about the wickedness that destroyed their fellow-Jews.

There are Christians who would agree with this, but none the less this is not the doctrine of forgiveness to be found in the New Testament. We all desperately need God's forgiveness, and to obtain this we ourselves must forgive those who have wronged us. According to Jesus's teaching, we cannot be forgiven unless we forgive. This is emphasised in the Lord's Prayer, in the only clause which was later enlarged upon: 'Forgive us the wrong we have done, as we have forgiven those who have wronged us . . . For if you forgive others the wrongs they have done, your heavenly Father will also forgive you; but if you do not forgive others, then the wrongs you have done will not be forgiven by your heavenly Father' (Matt. 6:12, 14f. NEB). The same point is made in the Epistles: 'Be ye kind to one another, tender-hearted, forgiving one another as God for Christ's sake forgave you' (Eph. 4:32). This applies to a grudge about injustice to others as much as the wrong done to ourselves. It holds, however terrible the wrong that has been done. Penitence and restitution (so far as this is possible) are required for God's forgiveness to be appropriated; but they are consequent on the assurance of our forgiveness rather than its ground. Without a change of heart a person who has done the wrong is unable to make the first move: if reconciliation is to be achieved, the persons wronged (or those who act on their behalf) must take the initiative. This does not simply apply to individuals, but also to whole groups who do evil or suffer injustice.

I think that the basic difference between the Jewish and Christian viewpoints here lies in a differing assessment of people's ability to change. According to the Jewish view, it is possible for a person to do this by an act of will. According to the Christian view, divine grace is needed to effect a real change of character, and so to be truly penitent. It needs to be recognised too that corporate penitence and corporate forgiveness are possible: it is not merely a matter for individuals (Shriver, 1995).

The need for dialogue

I am sure that there are many other differences between Christians and Jews. For example, Judaism is predominantly the religion of a particular race. Jews do not regard the Law of Moses as binding upon Gentiles. Christianity, on the other hand, is a worldwide religion which knows no national barriers. I have only tried to spotlight here the main theological differences between Jews and Gentiles. I have tried to state them as fairly as possible on both sides, and my intention is not to show that one side has more of the truth than the other (although of course as a Christian I espouse Christian beliefs) but rather to show that there are big gaps to be traversed for a Jew to become a Jewish Christian; and some of these are gaps of which he or she may not be fully aware until after a transition has been made.

I believe that there should be more dialogue between Christians and Jews on these theological themes. Of course there has been dialogue in the past, right back to the time of Origen and Eusebius in the early Church, and with Rabbi Abbahu of Caesarea. Dialogue continued in the Middle Ages, and later in Spain; but it was loaded in favour of Christians by reason of their dominance. As Schoeps puts it:

★ ★ ★

For nineteen centuries Jews and Christians have passed through the world together. There has been no lack of side glances, but true dialogue never developed, nor, in fact, could it develop. During the first centuries the Jewish side had no other interest other than refuting Christian interpretations of Jewish dialogues, holding themselves aloof from true encounter through 'refutations' of their opponent. When Christianity acceded to power, Christians no longer had any serious *desire* to engage in discussions with the Jews, for the latter's very impotence was seen as an overwhelming instance of God's judgement. (Schoeps, 1965)

However, in this century there have been some serious attempts at dialogue (Fry, 1996), the most notable of which was that between Martin Buber and the evangelical theologian Karl Ludwig Schmidt in 1933 under the auspices of the Jewish academy in Stuttgart. After the Holocaust attempts have been made to revive dialogue by the World Council of Churches with a quarterly newsletter issued by the Consultation on the Church and the Jewish People, but this has generally benefited only those concerned with ecumenism. I believe that there ought to be more serious discussion between Christians and Jews on the themes highlighted in this chapter; and I regret that this has not been put in hand by the Council of Christians and Jews. But dialogue was not the main reason for writing this book. Its object has been to show the gulf that exists between Jews and Christians, and the difficulties that a Jewish Christian faces in any attempt to bridge it. Fortunately the work of the Manor House Group of Jews and Christians has been made available to a wider public (Bayfield & Braybrooke, 1992). Among this group is a rabbi for whom I have a very great respect; Rabbi Albert Friedlander. I cannot help noticing, with some sadness, that in his contribution he writes with characteristic honesty:

We Jews talked to those Christians with whom we had most in common; and they in turn met Jewish scholars whose openness had made them participants with most religious discussions within the general community. What would have happened if we had brought Jewish Christians into this group? . . . I know that our discussions with them should not differ from our discussions with the Christians in our dialogue group; in practice there would be differences. (Friedlander, 1992)

O dear! We Jewish Christians still have a long way to go.

6

The Jews and the land

The biblical promise

I remember some twenty years ago accompanying a Southwark diocesan pilgrimage to the Holy Land when I was Bishop of Kingston upon Thames, and being made to have a disputation in Jerusalem with Professor Werblowsky. It was on the question of the land, and I was put up to argue that the Jewish faith did not require the Jews to possess the land of Israel. I'm afraid I was on a hiding to nothing. Looking back now, I can't think how I was persuaded to undertake the commission. If the Professor did not wipe the floor with me, that could have only been due to his courtesy!

Again and again in the Hebrew Scriptures the Jews, or rather the descendants of Abraham, are promised the Holy Land. God made a covenant with Abram (as he was then called) when he first entered Canaan, God appeared to him in a vision and is reported to have said: 'Unto thy seed will I gave this land' (Gen. 12:7). The promise is spelled out in a further vision by a 'covenant' or agreement with him, according to Genesis 15, in which God is reported to have said: 'To your descendants I give this land from the River of Egypt to the Great River, the river Euphrates, the territory of the Kenites, Kenizzites, Kadmonites, Hittites, Perizzites, Rephaim, Amorites, Canaanites, Girgashites, Hivites and Jebusites.' (Gen: 15.18–20 NEB). That promise was in fact only once completely fulfilled, in the reign of Solomon. Perhaps it is somewhat idealised here, but the verse represents the deeply felt belief that if Abraham's descendants were circumcised and were obedient to God's will, the land would be theirs, and it would be a land 'flowing with milk and honey'. These are by no means the only times when there is a reference to this promise; and in Deuteronomy 34:4 Moses before he died was allowed a glimpse of the land which he was not to be allowed himself to enter. Because of the disobedience of Israel during their exodus from Egypt, they were, according to the Pentateuch, made to wander in the wilderness for forty years before conquering their promised land. The book of Joshua gives an account of how the occupation took place. Historians have argued about the actual course of events; but what is undeniable is that the Jews did conquer the land and ruled it until Samaria fell to the Assyrians in the year 721 BC and Jerusalem fell to Babylon in 586 BC.

In June 1970 the General Synod of the Dutch Reformed Church adopted an extensive study document on 'Israel, People, Land and State'. It contains the best statement that I know about the relationship of the land to the people of Israel:

> In its faith Israel regarded its tie with the land as a unique one. It had no natural right to the land, and was not allowed to deal with it as if the land were its possession to which it could lay claim. It was the land allotted by God to his people, the land which God had already promised to the patriarchs. Even in a time when Israel already dwelt in the land and had possession of it, it remained 'the promised land', the gift of grace which was inexorably bound up with God's love. In other words, Israel was always convinced that the land was an essential element of the covenant.
>
> According to the entire OT in all its parts the chosen people and the promised land belong together, owing to God. The land was the place allotted to this people in order that they might realise their vocation as God's people to form a holy society. Again and again the prophets stress the point that the land is promised and given for the sake of this calling. When the people did not come up to their vocation as a chosen people, the

prophets threatened them with expulsion. Exile was understood by them as a sign of divine judgement, and return was understood by them as God's renewed gracious turning towards his people and as a new possibility, granted by him, for them to live according to their calling. Being allowed to dwell in the land could be regarded as a visible sign of God's election and as a concrete form of salvation.

We have said above that for Israel its election was no end in itself, but was directed towards the future: through the fulfilment of the destiny of the people of God and through what God does to his people, the nations also shall get to know God and turn to him. The dwelling of Israel in the land also partook of this directedness towards the future. This perspective in which the promised land is put comes clearly to the fore in the preaching of the prophets in the time of the exile. When they speak about the return to the land, they have in mind the historical situation; however, they speak in terms which go beyond the actual historical moment. It was the firm conviction of the people of the OT that they could reach their real destiny as God's covenant-people only in the land of Palestine, and that the realisation of this destiny was closely linked to the salvation of the world.

Thus according to the OT the land forms an essential part of the election by which God has bound himself to this particular people. Certainly the bond of God with his people is not severed when the people are outside the land, and certainly the people can live there also in quiet and peace, but the enforced separation of people and land is always something abnormal. There is no question of a separate election of the land; rather, it is a vital aspect of the election of Israel.

Jews in the Diaspora

Despite this close connection between land and people, it has to be said that many Jews have chosen to live outside Israel, and have shown no desire to return to their ancestral home. In fact, ever since the exile way back in Old Testament times, there have been more Jews living outside their ancestral home than within it. In New Testament times it has been calculated that there were eight million Jews, of whom one million lived in Palestine. Philo of Alexandria informs us that Jews comprised half the human race! Even allowing for exaggeration this suggests that there were a vast number of Jews in the Diaspora (the dispersion; Hebrew *galuth*), and that they must have been extraordinarily successful at proselytising (Feldman, 1993).

In Alexandria, which had established itself as the leading commercial and cultural centre of the Mediterranean, there was in the New Testament period an estimated population of a hundred and eighty thousand Jews. Cicero tells us, in defence of Flaccus, that the payment of the half shekel to the Temple treasury in Jerusalem by Jews in the Diaspora was so great that it upset the price of gold in the Roman world! Rome too was a great centre of Jewish population, although not so large as Alexandria. Julius Caesar gave the Jews special privileges there. In the reign of Tiberius, there was Jewish influence in high places. The Jewish king Agrippa played a leading part in arranging the succession of Claudius, and his son, Agrippa II, was actually brought up in Claudius's household. His sister Berenice became the mistress of the Emperor Titus.

The Jews in the Diaspora paid their dues to the Jewish Temple. They were supposed to visit it three times a year for the Jewish great festivals; but of course only a proportion of them did so. Apart from the Temple Tax, they showed no particular loyalty to their ancestral land, covenant or no covenant. When the Jewish revolt broke out in AD 66, the only Jews in the Diaspora who joined it was a contingent from Adabiene in Mesopotamia. Although Diaspora Jews were largely ignored by rabbis who lived in the Holy Land, there is no reason to believe that they were not observant, in the same kind of way as Jews who live in England may be deeply observant of their religious faith. Indeed at Elephantine in Upper Egypt they seem to have established a kind of temple of their own. In the second century AD there were savage revolts by Jews in Egypt, Cyrene, Cyprus and Mesopotamia, but generally speaking Diaspora Jews were comfortably established wherever they lived. Through their Jewish network, they had excellent communications throughout the Roman Empire, and so their trade prospered. The land may have been an essential part of the covenant with which God bound himself to his chosen people, but it was not so essential that they felt the need to resettle there. While in no way denying the theology of the land as expressed by the General Synod of the Dutch Reformed Church, as cited above, it has to be said that the majority of the Jews seem to have ignored it. At the same time, there were fiercely nationalist feelings among those who did live in the land, as the Jewish revolt of AD 66 shows.

The same attitude towards the Holy Land persisted among most Diaspora Jews this century until the Shoah and the end of the Second World War. Many Jews were comfortably established in lands which were predominantly Christian or Muslim. Elsewhere they were subject to disabilities and to persecution and poverty, and these longed for a place of refuge, but this did not manifest itself as a determination to return to the Holy Land. It is the same today in Western Europe, although a recent survey has disclosed dilemmas about Jewish identity in Britain, due to assimilation, 'marrying out', and general secularisation (Cooper and Morrison, 1991).

Zionism and its opponents

Zionism did not begin until the first Zionist Congress was held in Basle in 1894, as a result of Theodor Herzl's revulsion at the anti-Semitism which became apparent at the recent trial in France of Alfred Dreyfus. Earlier, however, in 1839, my forebear Sir Moses Montefiore, on the first of his seven pilgrimages to the Holy Land, wrote in his diary:

I sincerely pray that my journey may be beneficial to the Jews; not only to those who are already there, but to many others who may come to settle in the Holy Cities, either from love for the Land of Promise, or from a desire to quit countries where persecution prevents their living in peace. I shall then be amply repaid for the fatigue and anxiety of my journey (Loewe, 1983).

★   ★   ★

Moses Montefiore spoke before his time: he was a kind of Zionist before Zionism began – but at the same time he preferred to keep his residence in Britain. Conditions would have had to be pretty bad before a Jew opted to emigrate to the Holy Land. Sir Moses commented on the conditions there: 'I think the poverty of the Jews in Safed must be greater than anything that can be imagined in England or on the continent of Europe: it must be seen to be believed.'

The situation of the Jews under Turkish rule was indeed pitiable, and it is therefore not surprising that until the mid-twentieth century Zionism was not espoused by the majority of Jews in the dispersion. Even in Germany Jews showed no wish to emigrate to Palestine until the advent of Nazi persecution. Here in England in 1906 Arthur Balfour invited a young Russian Jewish scientist to meet him, and heard from Weissmann a reasoned and passionate exposition of the Zionist cause. 'It was from that meeting' Balfour later said, 'that I saw that the Jewish form of patriotism is unique' (Ecclestone, 1980). And of course it was out of that meeting that the Balfour Declaration eventually sprang during the First World War, when on 2 November 1917 the British Government issued a declaration of sympathy with Jewish Zionist aspirations, pledging support for 'the establishment in Palestine of a national home for the Jewish people'. The League of Nations Mandate for Palestine in 1922 incorporated the Balfour Declaration and explicitly stated that 'recognition has thereby been given to the historical connection of the Jewish people with Palestine and to the task of reconstituting their national home in that country', giving to Jews a national home in Palestine (of which Great Britain was given the mandate by the League of Nations after the First World War had ended).

My cousin Claude Montefiore, one of the founders in England of Liberal Judaism, was asked by Herzl to be his English Zionist lieutenant. He described Jews as like water in a sponge. The sponge could absorb a certain amount of water, but too much water made it drip. In the same way he believed that large concentrations of Jews in the Gentile word caused anti-Semitism. But Claude was not a Zionist, and he refused. He hoped for the assimilation of the Jews with the population of the respective countries of their birth, and for pure monotheism to spread from them to the world (Cohen, 1950). Discussing the mission of the Jews, he wrote:

> Why do we still believe in the continuing and unaccomplished mission? For several reasons. Mainly, I think, because our religion and religious experience have not yet become the religion and religious experience of all mankind, and we possess the faith that *in their essentials* they are destined to become so . . . The religious work which the Jewish brotherhood has to do did not cease at the birth of Christianity . . . That Christianity was intended by God to play a great religious part in the history of the world, I firmly believe; but I also believe that its appearance in the world did not betoken the end of Judaism as a religion of value. Christianity itself seems to Jews only a stage in the preparation of the world for a purified, developed and universalised Judaism (C. G. Montefiore, 1923).

It was this hope of a purified and universalised Judaism that led Claude Montefiore to reject Zionism.

The Balfour Declaration which granted Israel to the Jewish race as a homeland was shown to some half a dozen Jews, of whom Claude Montefiore was one of the two who were opposed to Zionism. In a lecture he gave later he said:

> We objected to the words because we denied that the Jews were any longer a nation, and we did not want them ever to become a nation again. We claimed and desired, as I and my friends still claim and desire, that they should be be free and equal citizens of all the countries in which they lived. We feared that the proposed national home might create more anti-semitism than it would cure. Our views and objections however were not listened to, except that for the definite article 'the' the indefinite article 'a' was substituted, so that the words now run 'a national home for the Jewish people' (Cohen, 1950).

★ ★ ★

I have no doubt that these objections were sincerely meant, and indeed it could be argued that Claude was right, and that the State of Israel has indeed caused more anti-Semitism, at least among Arab nations, than it can cure. Although the PLO, Egypt and Jordan have made peace with Israel, the Muslim world as a whole is hostile to Israel because Arab land has been occupied, Arab property has been confiscated, and Arabs are stripped of their political and human rights. At the same time there may have been some unconscious reasons for Claude's opposition to Zionism. Like his great uncle Moses, he was every inch an Englishman as well as a Jew, and it must be added that he never entertained the possibility of living in Palestine: he was very comfortably off, living on inherited English wealth.

Claude Montefiore was not alone in rejecting Zionism. Asher Ginsberg (ob. 1927) believed that there should be a Jewish community in Palestine, but that it should have a social, cultural and religious mission which would inspire Jews in the Diaspora. He did not look to a political State of Israel. Buber believed that the creation of a Jewish State would corrupt the mission of the Jews, because nationalism was incompatible with its spiritual message. Albert Einstein preferred agreement with Arabs so that Arabs and Jews could live together in peace to the establishment of a Jewish State. But this was not to be.

However, after the terrible events of the Shoah, Jews desperately needed a place of refuge, and that place was the land of Israel.

Israel's Declaration of Independence

The British found themselves in great difficulties trying to administer the Mandate, attempting to be fair to the Palestinian Jews already in possession of the land, and also to the Mandate which committed them to 'facilitate Jewish immigration' and 'close settlement by Jews on the land, including State lands and waste land'. Restrictive policies when hundreds of thousands of homeless Jews, survivors of the Nazi Holocaust, were trying to join their Jewish brethren, caused great tension and violence. There was terrorism by Arabs against Jews, and the Jews in turn set up Hagana, their defence organisation. There was violence against British attempts to control immigration. The position of the British became impossible. On 15 May 1948 the Mandate was terminated, and the independence of Israel was proclaimed.

At long last, after an interval of over two thousand years the Jews regained sovereignty over the Holy Land which they had lost way back in 63 BC when Pompey intervened in an internal Jewish squabble, entered the Holy of Holies in the Jewish Temple, and made Judaea a tributary of Rome. Even so the sovereignty that was then lost to Rome had only been in existence for a short period since 586 BC when the Jews were deported to Babylon. After the demise of the Babylonian Empire Judaea had fallen under Persian rule, under which Ezra returned to Jerusalem in 457 BC, closely followed by Nehemiah in 444 BC. The Persian Empire later fell to Alexander the Great, and at his death the Jews came under the rule of the Seleucid dynasty based in Syria. As a result of the Maccabean revolt, Israel finally obtained political independence in 129 BC. It was lost again, as we have seen, in 63 BC, so that since 586 BC it only achieved it for a mere sixty-six years.

The Roman rule of Judaea passed to Byzantium, until in AD 614 Persians entered Jerusalem, but in 619 the Byzantines counter-attacked and returned. By 638 the Arabs had seized the Holy City. They were succeeded by the Seljuks in 1072, the Crusaders in 1099, the Marmelukes in 1291, and the Ottoman Turks from 1517 until 1917, and after the First World War the League of Nations, as we have noted, gave the mandate of government to the British. After all that period of occupation, and successive occupying powers, it is not surprising that there was great rejoicing among Jews when at long last the independence of Israel was proclaimed.

This independence was won at some cost and with what seemed to outsiders great ruthlessness (Grollenberg, 1979). Palestinian Arabs fled before the Jews, and established themselves in neighbouring countries in huge refugee camps. They lost the land which they had held for centuries. Some land had already been purchased under the banner of Zionism in the last quarter of the nineteenth century, and now fresh land was seized whose Arab owners had fled. Nearly a million Palestinians left the country as hundreds of thousands of Jews entered the country. More land became cultivated, and towns and industries were built. The young State was kept going by external help from Jews in the Diaspora, especially in the United States of America, where nearly six million Jews live. (The State of Israel has developed a special relationship with the government of the USA, with much military aid.) There has arisen intense Jewish nationalism. All had to undertake military service. Surrounding Arab states sought to reverse the situation. Although armistices were signed in 1949, armed warfare between Jews and Arabs erupted on two occasions. As a result of the victory of the Jews in 1967 in the Six Days War, there are today 'occupied territories' around Gaza and on the West Bank of the Jordan, and in one part of Jerusalem itself. A small amount of territory has recently been returned to the Palestinians for Arafat's Palestinian Authority to administer; but the situation is very tense and gives rise to spasmodic violence.

At its Sixth Assembly in 1983 the World Council of Churches reaffirmed principles it had previously enunciated by which it believed that a peaceful settlement of the Israeli–Palestine conflict could be reached. It took note of the United Nations Resolution 242 and suggested that all revisions of that resolution should ensure:

a) the withdrawal of Israeli troops from all territories occupied in 1967;
b) the right of all states, including Israel and the Arab states, to live in peace with secure and recognised boundaries;
c) the implementation of the rights of the Palestinians to self-determination, including the right of establishing a sovereign Palestinian State.

This resolution, however, took no account of whether Israel's boundaries are defensible without its retention of at least some of the occupied territories. The second occupation of the Holy Land by the Jews in some ways replicated what had happened under the first occupation under Joshua. Great injustice took place then. There was much ruthless fighting and the Israelites' enemies were put to the sword, including the *herem*, which was a form of genocide with the wholesale destruction of people and cattle. There was treachery too when the prostitute Rahab enabled Jericho to be captured (her name is even celebrated in the New Testament in the Epistle to the Hebrews). The first occupation of the Holy Land spelled grave suffering and indeed injustice to the inhabitants who stood in the way of the invaders; the Kenites and the Kenizzites, and the Kadmonites, and the Hittites, and the Perizzites and the Rephaim and the Amorites and the Canaanites and the Jebusites whom the Jews displaced. Nobody, however, accuses the Jews of wrongdoing in their earlier occupation of the Promised Land, partly because in those far off days there were no rules of warfare, and partly because the land had been promised to them through the election of God. If that promise still holds today, it is perhaps not altogether surprising that in their reconquest of the land the behaviour of the Jews has not been altogether different from what it had been in the distant past. Once again the point has been well put by the General Synod of the Dutch Reformed Church:

> Because of the special place of the Jewish people, we endorse in the present situation the right of existence of the State of Israel. On the other hand we wonder whether this special state does not also make the right questionable. First of all we remember the way in which the state came into existence in 1948. This took place in a human, all too human way, as is the case with practically every other state; all kinds of political means and often means of violence have been used. But the Jewish people have never been better than other peoples. The entry into the land under Joshua and the return under Nehemiah were, morally speaking, dubious affairs too. The special place of Israel was never based on its moral qualities, but solely on what in the OT is called God's righteousness, that is, his unmerited, steadfast covenant-love. This love can never be a licence to sin. But it is not annulled by sin either. Therefore we ought not to dispute on

moral grounds the right of the State of Israel to exist. Otherwise we would have to ask ourselves how we ourselves can stand before God.

At the same time it must be remembered how in the Old Testament the canonical prophets gave warning of exile as a result of the sins of the people and their disobedience to God and neglect of his covenant. When one considers how the divine ordinances about the treatment of aliens – I refer to Palestinians – are being ignored today in Israel and the occupied territories, it is not altogether impossible that this situation could recur.

The Zionist movement, as it developed, was primarily (and understandably) a secular movement seeking a place of refuge and a national home for a terribly persecuted people. As a result, the State of Israel calls itself a secular State, although there is no written constitution and Orthodox Jewry has special privileges there (not unlike those of the Roman Catholic Church in Eire), and small Orthodox political parties are of great importance in forming coalition governments, exercising influence out of all proportion to their numbers by holding the balance of power.

The first harbinger of Zionism would not have agreed with its secular status. He was Moses Hess, a socialist thinker, at one time fascinated by Karl Marx. However he believed that socialism should not be based merely on economics and technology but on the spirit. In 1855 he published *Rome and Jerusalem* in which he stressed that the Kingdom of God was not in heaven but on earth, and that in order to fulfil its worldwide destiny of bringing in God's Kingdom the Jewish people needed land where it could have have an independent and self-determining existence. 'He died before the movement had even started. But even today, seventy five years after his death, the Zionist movement has not yet really caught up with him' (Buber, 1952).

The real founders of the movement were Leo Pinsker and Theodor Hertzl. Pinsker was a doctor and rationalist who lived in Odessa, and who was much shaken by the first Russian pogroms. Hertzl was a Viennese writer, who was startled by the anti-Semitism manifested in the French Dreyfus affair, as we have noted. Pinsker sought a homeland, a fatherland, a plot of land where Jews could live as human beings. However, homelands and fatherlands are not sought so much as given as an inheritance. It did not matter where it lay, so Pinsker thought, so long as it was a refuge. However, Palestine had an emotional appeal for people, but he did not think that Jews should aim at restoring the old Judaea. He settled for Palestine because that is what people wanted, and because it was a realisable ideal; but he believed that people only wanted to return to Palestine because it would give them a refuge and a home.

Herzl was at the start even more ambiguous about the choice of Palestine for a national home. He even played with the British Government's suggestion of Uganda; but later his choice lay between Palestine and the Argentine where Baron Hirsch, who contributed huge sums of money, was promoting the settlement of Jews. (Today there are as many as a quarter of a million Jews settled in the Argentine, but it was also a country to which Nazis fled, so that today there still exists a virulent anti-Semitism.) Herzl settled on Palestine as his place of refuge in his book *The Jewish State*, after a visit to London when he had met some prominent English Jews and Sir Samuel Montagu had suggested 'one might offer the Sultan two million pounds for Palestine' (Buber, 1952). Herzl rightly believed that Palestine had a large emotional appeal to the Jewish masses. It was on these grounds that he sold the idea of a Jewish national home in the Holy Land. The fact that it was a Holy Land, bound to the Jewish people by God in a solemn covenant, did not enter into his argument. There were of course later thinkers, such as Asher Ginsberg and Rabbi Abraham Kook, who understood this; but with such a secular origin to the Zionist movement, it is hardly surprising that Israel at its independence called itself a secular State.

Jewish supremacy in the Holy Land today

Fundamentalist Jews, such as *Gush Emunim*, disapprove of secular Zionism because they believe that the land of Israel belongs to the

Jews by the gift from God, and therefore it is not to be regarded as a place of refuge but as the Promised Land; and they are thus intransigent on the question of Jewish sovereignty. Other very Orthodox Jews (the Hasidic sects of Satma and Notera Karta) hold that there can be no valid State of Israel until the coming of the Messiah. Whatever people's views may be, the fact is that, after the Israeli victory in the Six Days War in 1967, some three million Arabs now live under Israeli control. Nearly a million live in the State of Israel, where they enjoy citizenship rights, but complain that they are in fact second-class citizens, subject to restrictions and at times violence from the police. In the Gaza strip, where there is great poverty and unemployment, there live 813,000 Arabs, while 1.32 million live on the West Bank. In the towns they now enjoy limited autonomy in police, education, public health, under the interim agreements under the Oslo accords. This autonomy applies only to the towns. In the West Bank and Gaza there have been built (illegitimately under international law) fourteen urban settlements and eighty-two rural settlements where some 128,000 Jews live. Arabs yearn for an independent Palestinian State where they can enjoy freedom, dignity, a passport, and political and civil rights under their own government. Jews and Arabs are living in the same areas, but 90 per cent of the cultivable land, 75 per cent of the water and all the infrastructure is geared to support the Jews (Tutunji and Khaldi, 1997). Israel may confiscate Palestinian property in the name of the 'public interest' to establish settlements, but Arab property owners are ineligible on account of their ethnicity and religion to own or rent a single housing development on their land. A large number of West Bank Arabs earn their living in Israel, but due to restrictions they have difficulty in gaining access to Jerusalem. East Jerusalem which used to be Arab has been annexed by Israel (illegitimately under international law). Two hundred thousand Israeli settlers live there, and with the further building of settlements such as that in Ha Hamor there will be more.

Jews, however, believe it is vital for their own security and protection against terrorism that they make these regulations which restrict the rights of Arabs, and defend on these grounds the violence

that they sometimes have to use. But Arabs argue that their
opposition to Jewish controls is due to their unfairness and to the
violence which Arabs suffer and have suffered at the hands of the
Jewish authorities. Certainly there are on record some extreme
instances of such violence. Why, for example, did Israeli troops stand
guard outside the Palestinian refugee camps called Sabra and Satila
in 1982 while so-called Lebanese Christian Militia butchered the
inhabitants and then bulldozed their bodies into mass graves? That
was some time ago; but much more recently an equally disturbing
incident occurred. In April 1996 a Lebanese boy was killed by an
Israeli booby trap in South Lebanon, and in retaliation the Hizbollah
launched rockets across the Lebanese border against Israel. Israel
responded with a three-week blitz on Southern Lebanon, during
which the Israelis launched a 17-minute attack on the United
Nations base at Qana, killing at least 109 refugees in the camp,
including 55 children. The Israelis claimed that this was a mistake,
but the United Nations has concluded that this was not the case.
During these hostilities a caption appeared in an Israeli newspaper
which was unwittingly ironical: 'Israeli soldiers briefly halt their
shelling to commemorate Holocaust Day'. Some Jews, both in Israel
and in the USA, have formed human rights movements to draw
attention to Israel's treatment of non-Jews in its midst and on its
borders.

There are other countries where minorities are treated grossly
unfairly, and where dreadful massacres have been committed; and
yet the world passes them by. Why then is such a fuss made about
the Jews' treatment of Arabs? Is this yet another case of widespread
anti-Semitism? Perhaps it is in part. But it is also true that the Jews
do constitute a special case. The land is only theirs by reason of a
covenant with God, and that covenant specifies obedience to the
laws of God by the Jewish people which are breached by their
treatment of non-Jews. This in no way exonerates other countries
for their treatment of minorities. It does, however, explain why
there is so often a spotlight upon Jewish practice.

Once again the position is well put by the Declaration of the
General Synod of the Dutch Reformed Church:

* * *

We maintain that whoever accepts for the Jewish people a role of their own among the nations must also in view of the political problems in and around Palestine accept for this people a right to a state of their own. This acceptance is based on the lasting tie with the land in view of the promise . . .

In speaking of Israel's unfaithfulness to its special calling, we did not assume that we are better than the Jews. We are only too conscious of the fact that we too as Christians, as churches, as so-called Christian states have repeatedly been guilty of discrimination, inhumanity and impermissible forms of nationalism. If Israel were a state like other states, we could not judge it by standards which no other state meets. But we believe that Israel is unique; its nature is based on God's election, for the Jews are still that special people which by God's promises is tied to this particular land. Therefore we expect from this people more than we expect from other people. He who is placed in a special position has to act in a special manner.

Jerusalem

If Israel is in a special position, then Jerusalem is a very special place. It is hallowed by Israel as its ancestral capital, and by the belief that 'the Lord has chosen Zion and desired it for his home' (Ps. 132:13). Some radical Jewish groups want to rebuild the Temple. The area is hallowed by Muslims because Mahommed is believed to have ascended into heaven from the Dome of the Rock, which is built upon the old Temple courts. And it is hallowed by Christians because it is the place where Jesus Christ was crucified, and rose again from the dead. It is thus a thrice holy city, and that makes its future all the more difficult and problematical. Muslims are being eased out (and in some cases forced out) of the Eastern quarter where they used to be in a majority, and a passageway has been opened up under the Dome of the Rock. Jews wish to make Jerusalem the capital of Israel, and already embassies are moving there from Tel Aviv. Christians have been particularly concerned with free access to the Holy Places, which by tradition are under the custody of the Franciscans.

The Fifth Assembly of the World Council of Churches held in Nairobi in 1975 affirmed that 'Jerusalem is a Holy City for three monotheistic religions: Judaism, Christianity and Islam. The tendency to minimise the importance for any of these three religions should be avoided.' The Sixth Assembly at Vancouver in 1983 reaffirmed this, and emphasised that the special legislation known as the Status Quo of the Holy Places must be safeguarded and confirmed in any agreement concerning Jerusalem. The Council called the attention of the churches to the need for:

- actions which will ensure a continuing indigenous Christian presence in Jerusalem;
- wider ecumenical awareness of the plight of the indigenous Muslim and Christian communities suffering from the repressive action of the occupying power in East Jerusalem and other occupied territories.

The Sixth Assembly also called upon all the churches to express their common concern that although Israeli law guarantees free access for members of all religious traditions rooted in Jerusalem to their holy places, the state of war between Israel and Arab States, the political reality caused by the annexation of East Jerusalem and the continuing occupation of the West Bank mean that Arab Muslims and Christians continue to experience serious difficulties and are often prevented from visiting the Holy City.

These concerns, first voiced in 1983, are even graver today than they were fifteen years ago. The issue of Jerusalem raises the same basic problems as those concerning the land of Israel, but over Jerusalem they are raised in a more acute form.

It has not been my concern, in writing this chapter, to give my own views on this tragic situation. I shall do this in the final chapter of this book when I give a personal viewpoint. Here I am concerned only to set out the facts, the theology and the pronouncements of churches on matters concerning the Land of Israel. It has been necessary to do this, because a Jewish Christian, like any other Jew, feels an emotional pull to the land of his forefathers, however distant they may be, and at the same time because he is a Christian he can stand back from the situation a little and view it as it were from without.

Additional note on Jewish population today in Israel and the Diaspora

Before the last World War it was estimated that there were about seventeen million Jews, of which ten million lived in Europe, over five million in the Americas, 830,000 in Asia, 600,000 in Africa and 33,000 in Australasia.

Today, after the Holocaust, it is reckoned that there are some fourteen million Jews, which include four and a half million in Israel (including East Jerusalem and the West Bank settlements), one and a half million in the former USSR, and nearly seven million in the Americas. Countries with large Jewish populations include USA (5,800,000), France (600,000), Canada (360,000) UK (300,000), Argentine (250,000), South Africa (114,000), Brazil (100,000).

These figures are taken from the *Jewish Yearbook*, 1996.

Jewish and Christian liturgies

If you want to find out something about the spirituality of a religion, look at its liturgies. Of course the tradition of private prayer is just as important; but at the same time a liturgy will tell you a great deal about the ethos of a religion. It will disclose which beliefs it holds most dear, and what are its enduring features. Liturgies change little over the centuries, and even new forms of worship usually show strong continuity with their predecessors. Liturgies also engage the feelings and make a strong impression on the memory and they are therefore of importance in the formation of spirituality. Although I have not been using the Jewish liturgy for well over half a century, it has made an enduring impression upon me and has helped to form my spirituality as a Jewish Christian. It is therefore important to me, and I cannot explain myself without comparing and contrasting it with Christian liturgies, sometimes to the advantage of the one, and sometimes to the advantage of the other.

There are many differences between Christian and Jewish liturgies. First and foremost, Jewish worship is non-sacramental. There are no sacraments in Judaism. Circumcision is a sign of the covenant, not 'an outward and visible sign of an inward and spiritual grace given to us'. Sometimes the use of bread and wine for the sanctification of the Sabbath in the Kiddush on the eve of the

Sabbath is compared to the Christian Eucharist with its common use of bread and wine; but in fact there is no similarity, except for the fact that, if the Last Supper did not take place on Passover Eve as the Synoptic Gospels record (and as seems probable to me), then it may have been a Kiddush at which Jesus set aside bread and wine for sacramental use (although this would not explain how he took the cup 'after supper'). But this would in no sense make Kiddush into a sacrament. Personally, I find sacramental worship a wonderful blessing, and I feel that Jewish liturgies are greatly weakened by a lack of sacraments. For these provide an objectivity in worship which otherwise can so much depend upon our changeable feelings.

When we come to compare the public worship of Orthodox Jews and Christians in the Catholic tradition, we find that, although there are differences, there are also similarities. The reading or chanting of the psalms plays a large part in the liturgies of both Faiths. In both there is a reading from Scripture. In both there are confessions of sin and ascriptions of praise, albeit in differing proportions. And some ancient Christian prayers are derived, it would seem, from their even more ancient Jewish predecessors.

The Morning Service

In the Roman Catholic and Orthodox Churches the Eucharist has been the main and indeed the only service of worship on a Sunday morning. Until recently in the Church of England, when Parish Communion became the norm in the parish church, Morning Prayer was the main service. Together with Evening Prayer, it was composed by Archbishop Cranmer from a combination of mediaeval offices. His service opens with a long confession of sins, followed by the singing or saying of psalms, readings from the Old and New Testaments, prayers and probably a sermon. According to the Jewish rite Morning Service is the only liturgy on a Saturday morning. It requires a *minyan* or religious quorum of ten males. Some of the prayers are very ancient in origin. The institution of public prayer among the Jews is said to have begun in the time of Ezra the Scribe, after Jews had returned from exile in Babylon, when the original Temple was still in ruins and had not been rebuilt. After the destruction of Herod's Temple in AD 70, the synagogue was the only focus for all Jewish communal worship. Prayers were added from other later sources, but the Sephardi prayer book is thought to be Palestinian in origin. I have used here the Sephardi rather than the Ashkenazi rites, because I am more familiar with the former. There are differences, but not in essentials.

Jewish Morning service for the Sabbath has its focus in the reading of a set portion of the Pentateuch (*parasha*), split into seven smaller sections with a Cohen (priest), Levi (if one is available) and five laymen 'called up' to the *tebah* (reading desk) to be present as the Minister chants from the Torah. This focal point of the service is followed by the *Haftorah*, which is chanted by a lay person (and this may be someone under thirteen before he has been *barmitzvah*). It consists of a chanted reading from the prophets. The service begins and ends with prayers, psalms and short readings from the Scriptures (all but one from the Pentateuch) and excerpts from the Mishnah and Talmud. There is usually no sermon, which is just as well, as Morning Service for the Sabbath is a really long service, and takes up forty-eight pages of my Sephardi Prayer Book, the first eighteen pages of which come from the daily morning service! It comprises in addition to many prayers seven short bible readings, eighteen psalms, four excerpts from the Mishnah, three from the Talmud and one from the Sifra. I'm afraid that I have never attended the whole service. We used to appear about 11 a.m. when it was well under way. Morning Service is the main service on the Sabbath. (There is also an Afternoon Service and a Concluding Service). It involves removing the *Sepher Torah* (scroll of the Law) from the *echal* (Ark) and carrying it in procession to the *tebah*, where the portions of the day are read. This does not happen in the Afternoon Service for the Sabbath (a mere eleven pages), nor in the Concluding Service for the Sabbath (twenty-nine pages, including the whole of Psalm 119!). There is also a daily Morning and Evening Service. The service appears to have little structure (rather as I used to find

the service of Holy Communion in Cranmer's version in the Book
of Common Prayer)

I must not give too enthusiastic an impression of the Orthodox
version of this service, for it contains readings which strike us as
very strange today. Often in Jewish liturgy there are reminiscences
of Temple worship in the old days. For instance, every morning an
excerpt from the Talmud is read in explanation of the way in which
incense was made for use in the temple;

> The Rabbis have taught how the mixture of the incense was
> made; it contained three hundred and sixty eight manehs [one
> maneh equalled a hundred shekels]; three hundred and sixty five
> were according to the days of the solar year; and of the three
> remaining manehs, the high priest was to take his hands full, on
> the Day of Atonement . . . It was composed of eleven sorts of
> spices; balm, cloves, galbanum, frankincense, of each an equal
> weight, that is to say, seventy manehs; myrrh, cassia, spikenard,
> saffron, of each an equal weight, sixteen manehs, costus, twelve
> manehs; the rind of an odoriferous tree, three manehs, cinnamon,
> nine manehs, soap of Carsina, nine kabs, wine of Cyprus, three
> seahs . . .

And so on.

The main characteristics of Jewish worship are quite different
from this extract from the Talmud: they consist of joy, praise, and
thanksgiving. These elements are sadly and strangely lacking from
most Christian liturgical rites (with the possible exception of the
Orthodox Church's liturgy). Jewish worship has, I believe, a lot to
teach Christians here. Jews thank God by blessing him for his good
gifts. Morning service begins with a whole series of blessings. Some
of them show the very conservative nature of all liturgy. The first
blessing, for example, is evidently to be dated centuries before the
introduction of alarm clocks: 'Blessed art thou, O Lord, King of the
universe, who givest to the cock intelligence, to distinguish between
day and night.' Blessings include some which grate upon modern
ears. 'Blessed art thou, O Lord, King of the Universe, who hast not

made me a heathen ... who hast not made me a slave ... (for women) who hast made me according to thy will ... (for men) who hast not made me a woman.' (In the 1958 edition of the Sephardi prayer book, the English translation of the last named is understandably mistranslated, as in the American Jewish prayer book, to 'who hast set upon me the responsibilities of a man', although the original Hebrew remains unaltered!) In the Sephardi worship in which I was brought up, women are still exiled to the gallery and play no part in the liturgy, but not in Reformed and Liberal synagogues.

It would be wrong to concentrate on these particular blessings. Here is a better example of the many Jewish liturgical prayers which are so full of thanksgiving:

The breath of all living shall praise thy name, O Lord our God! And the spirit of all flesh shall continually glorify and extol thy memorial, O God our King! for thou art God from everlasting to everlasting; and beside thee we have neither king nor redeemer nor saviour, to redeem, deliver answer and pity us in all times of trouble and distress; we have no king to aid and support us but thee. God of the first and the last ages, God of all creatures, Lord of all generations, who is extolled with all manner of praise; who guideth his world with tenderness and his creatures with mercy. 'The Lord is ever awake, he neither slumbereth nor sleepeth.' But it is thou that rousest those who sleep, awakeneth those who slumber; revivest the dead, healest the sick, openest the eyes of the blind, and raisest those who are bowed down. Thou makest the dumb to speak, and revealest hidden things; and therefore unto thee alone do we give thanks.

Were our mouths filled with sacred song as the sea is with water, our tongues with shouting loudly as the roaring billows, our lips with praise as the widely-spread firmament; our eyes sparkling like the sun or the moon; our hands spread out as the eagle's wings in the skies; and our feet as swift as the hind's; we should yet be unable to thank thee sufficiently, O Lord our God! or adequately to bless thy name, O our King! for even one of the many thousands and ten thousands of benefits which thou hast vouchsafed to us and our ancestors, or the signs and wonders which didst perform aforetime; for thou, O Lord our God, didst redeem us from Egypt, and release us from the house of bondage; in time of famine thou didst feed us, and in plenty sustain us. Thou didst deliver us from the sword, save us from the pestilence, and relieve us from many sore diseases. Hitherto thy tender mercies have supported us, and thy kindness hath not forsaken us; and therefore the limbs which thou hast branched out in us, the spirit and soul which thou has breathed into our nostrils, and the tongue which thou has placed into our mouth; lo! they shall continually give thanks, bless, praise, glorify and sing unto thy name, O our King! for every mouth shall give thanks unto thee, every tongue shall praise thee, and every eye wait for thee. Unto thee shall every knee bend, and those of high stature shall bow down before thee. Every heart shall fear thee and the inward parts and reins shall sing praise unto thy name; as it is written: 'All my bones shall say, O Lord, who is like unto thee?'

A long prayer, somewhat fulsome, but surely a remarkable one, breathing thanksgiving and praise which comes from a full heart. There is nothing like it in the Book of Common Prayer, or the Alternative Service Book, or for that matter in the Roman Catholic Missal. I wish there were.

The idea of the superabundant blessings of God surfaces in the Seder night service for Passover Eve, in the *dayenu* prayer (meaning 'It would be sufficient for us'). The prayer starts: 'How numerous are the degrees of beneficence that the Lord hath conferred on us. For if he had brought us out of Egypt, but had not executed justice on the Egyptians, *dayenu*, it would have been sufficient for us.' It continues in a similar vein with another thirteen such clauses. (My mother, in refusing a second helping of food, had a tendency to say simply *dayenu*.) In the Jewish liturgy, even the prayer for the dead (*Kaddish*) begins with a blessing: 'May his great name be exalted and sanctified, who will hereafter renew the world, and quicken the dead . . .' Another pleasing characteristic of the Jewish Prayer

Book is a list of blessings for various occasions. I don't suppose that they are often used, but I find them charming. Thus, on seeing a rainbow: 'Blessed art thou, O Lord our God! King of the Universe; who rememberest the covenant, art true to thy covenant, and steadfast in thy word.' (The covenant is the one made with Noah after the flood.) Or again, on smelling aromatic fruit, such as lemons or citrons or apples: 'Blessed art thou, O Lord our God! King of the universe; who impartest a sweet smell to fruit,' and on hearing bad news: 'Blessed art thou, O Lord our God! King of the universe, who art a righteous judge.'

This emphasis on thanksgiving is not wholly absent from Christian worship. There is the prayer of General Thanksgiving, seldom used in Anglican worship in England, alas, but always used by Anglicans in the United States of America. Again, the central prayer in the Christian Eucharist is the Prayer of Thanksgiving, beginning 'It is very meet, right and our bounden duty that we should at all times and in all places give thanks unto thee . . .' (with an equivalent phrase in the new rites); but this note of thanksgiving is totally absent from the Prayer of Consecration in the Book of Common Prayer, and only implicitly present in the Alternative Service Book.

By way of contrast, the note of penitence and confession of sins is highly marked in the Book of Common Prayer, and still strongly present (if rather toned down) in the Alternative Service Book. For example, it has seemed to many that Cranmer must have suffered from a terribly guilty conscience when he composed the confession found in the service of Holy Communion in the Prayer Book):

Almighty God, Father of our Lord Jesus Christ, Maker of all things, Judge of all men; We acknowledge and bewail our manifold sins and wickedness, Which we, from time to time, most grievously have committed, By thought, word and deed, Against thy divine majesty, Provoking most justly thy wrath and indignation against us. We do earnestly repent, And are heartily sorry for these our misdoings; The remembrance of them is grievous unto us; The burden of them is intolerable. Have mercy upon us, Have mercy upon us, most merciful Father; For thy Son our Lord Jesus Christ's sake, Forgive us all that is past; And grant that we may ever hereafter Serve and please thee In newness of life, To the honour and glory of thy Name; Through Jesus Christ our Lord.

This note of abject penitence is much muted in Sabbath worship according to Jewish rites. After all, the Sabbath is a time for joy, not sorrow. In the long morning service there are only two brief prayers for forgiveness. One is used only during the 'Ten Penitential Days' in the *Amidah*, a long and very ancient prayer of thanksgiving and supplication. The addition contains the phrase 'Let slanderers have no hope and all apostates and froward ones perish as in a moment' (That includes me! It is a relic of the prayer added to the Eighteen Benedictions against Jewish Christians way back in the first century AD.) But lest we Christians feel superior, we must remember that the Book of Common Prayer contains a somewhat pejorative reference to Jews in its Good Friday collect, only slightly toned down in the Alternative Services Book. During these ten days of penitence the Amidah contains also the following prayer for forgiveness:

Forgive us, O our Father, for we have sinned; and pardon us, O our King, for we have transgressed; for thou, O God, art good and forgiving. Blessed art thou, O gracious Lord, who doest abundantly pardon.

The daily Morning Service includes plenty of penitence on Mondays and Thursdays. Whenever it is said, the following prayer for forgiveness is included:

May it be thy will, O Lord our God and the God of our fathers, to have compassion on us, to pardon all our sins, to forgive all our iniquities and to grant us remission for all our transgressions; and that the holy Temple may be speedily rebuilt in our days, that we may offer before thee the continual burnt-offering, that may atone for us: as thou hast prescribed in thy Law, by the hand of thy servant Moses . . .

★ ★ ★

However, most Jews do not really want the Temple rebuilt, so this part of the prayer might perhaps seldom come from the heart; but there is no reason to doubt the sincerity of the first part, asking for forgiveness. None the less it is the only mention of sin during the whole of Morning Prayer.

The Day of Atonement

The most solemn day in the Christian year is Good Friday, when Christians reflect upon the death of Jesus Christ upon the Cross, and what his self-sacrifice means for the world and for them. (Most Christians will be unable to do this nowadays, since Good Friday, which used to be for most people a holiday, is in these secular times now a normal working day.) Although there is no official Christian doctrine of atonement, the Nicene Creed speaks of Jesus who 'for us men and for our salvation came down from heaven . . . and was crucified for us under Pontius Pilate'. Traditionally one of the ways the sacrifice of Jesus is understood in the New Testament is as the fulfilment of what was attempted on the Day of Atonement. Christ is not the Jewish High Priest who ministered in the Jewish Temple, but the High Priest according to the order of Melchizedek who ministers in the heavenly Temple. There is no special rite for Anglicans on Good Friday, although a three-hour meditation on the Words of Jesus from the Cross as recorded in the Gospels has been a popular devotion since Victorian times. The Liturgical Commission has lately issued special forms of devotion for the 'Mass of the Pre-sanctified' on Good Friday, including a revised form of the 'Reproaches' which are customarily sung on that day and which in their old form could be interpreted in an anti-Jewish manner.

Good Friday is an occasion which in the bad old days Jews learnt to fear, for it gave rise to the charge they were deicides in having Jesus put to death. Even today this is the revised collect in the Alternative Services book:

★ ★ ★

Merciful God,
who made all men and hate nothing that you have made;
you desire not the death of a sinner
but rather that he should be converted and live.
Have mercy upon your ancient people the Jews,
and upon all who have not known you,
or who deny the faith of Christ crucified;
take from them all ignorance, hardness of heart and contempt
for your word,
and so fetch them home to your fold
that they may be made one flock under one shepherd,
through Jesus Christ our Lord.

The collect seems to assume that all Jews who are not Jewish Christians suffer from either ignorance, hardness of heart or contempt for God's Word. That is horrible. It is not the case.

Originally when the Jewish Temple was still standing, the High Priest on the Day of Atonement would go inside the veil of the Temple to the Holy Place to make atonement with the blood of a bull and a goat, and a second goat (the scapegoat) would be loosed into the wilderness, to bear the sins of the people. With the destruction of the Temple, sacrifice had to be discontinued, and prayer was substituted for it. So the Day of Atonement became a fast day for all Jews, filled with penitence and prayer. The Jewish liturgy reserves a full statement of guilt and repentance for a great 'orgy' of confession on this day. Some of the prayers can even outrival Cranmer's effusions in their expressions of guilt and penitence. There is one I remember vividly and can even recite in Hebrew. As one beats one's breast, one says 'Ashamnoo, bagadnoo, gazalnoo . . .' In Hebrew this prayer forms an 'alphabetical acrostic', that is to say, each clause starts with a letter of the alphabet, starting at the beginning with the first letter 'aleph. Here is a translation:

We have trespassed, we have dealt treacherously, we have robbed, we have spoken slander, we have committed iniquity, we have done wickedly, we have acted presumptuously, we have committed violence, we have forged falsehood, we have counselled evil, we have uttered lies, we have scoffed, we have rebelled, we have blasphemed, we have revolted, we have acted perversely, we have transgressed, we have oppressed, we have been stiff-necked, we have acted wickedly, we have corrupted, we have done abominably, we have gone astray ourselves and have caused others to err; we have turned aside from thy good precepts and commandments, and we heeded them not; 'But thou art just concerning all that has come upon us; for thou hast dealt most truly but we have done wickedly.'

You might think that this was quite enough, but the prayer goes on:

What shall we say before thee, O Thou who dwellest on high? or what shall we declare unto thee, who rulest above the skies? Behold, thou knowest the secret things as well as the revealed; thou knowest the secrets of the world, and the most hidden mysteries of all living; thou searchest the inward parts, and triest the reins and the heart; there is nothing concealed, neither is there anything hidden from thy sight. May it be thy will, O Lord our God, and the God of our fathers, to have mercy on us, to pardon our sins, to forgive our iniquities, and to pardon and forgive our transgressions.

The prayer continues, and there are others in a similar vein; but I feel that I have quoted enough! But it must not be forgotten that the Morning Service for the Day of Atonement also contains many prayers of praise and thanksgiving to God as well as those expressing contrition for sins.

The Funeral Service

To write about penitence and prayers for forgiveness brings to mind the service for the burial of the dead. A funeral service needs to bring together the sorrows of friends and relatives and to express our convictions about death and the future life, as well as gratitude for the good things in the life that has now ended. A funeral is an emotional occasion, and the liturgy needs to be sensitively worded.

The old Requiem Mass of the Roman Catholic Church was anything but a joyful service, and one felt that anyone was exceedingly lucky to escape the pains of hell. But this has been entirely remedied in that Church's new rite. The funeral service of the Anglican rite in the Book of Common Prayer has only one note of thanksgiving, and that of a somewhat negative kind: 'We give thee hearty thanks that it hath pleased thee to deliver this our brother out of the miseries of this sinful world . . .' There is one positive quotation from the Book of Revelation: 'Blessed are the dead which die in the Lord', and the minister does use the phrase 'sure and certain hope of the resurrection to eternal life' at the solemn moment of interment, but not before he has also said: 'In the midst of life we are in death: of whom may we seek for succour but from thee, O Lord, who for our sins art most justly displeased . . .' The tone is somewhat lightened in the new funeral rite in the Alternative Service Book, but there is little expression of joy and thanksgiving. With this may be contrasted the Funeral Service according to the Sephardi Jewish Prayer Book. The funeral takes place very soon after death, as is necessary in hot climates. The coffin has to be very simple. As seven circuits are made around the bier some beautiful verses are recited. As the words are unlikely to be known to non-Jewish readers, they are quoted here in full, despite their length:

I

Have mercy upon him, we beseech thee, O Lord, the living God, and King of the universe; for with thee is the fountain of life.'And continually may he walk in the land of life, and may his soul rest in the bond of life.'

2

May the Gracious One, in the abundance of his mercy, forgive his transgressions; may his good deeds be before his eyes, and may he be near unto God with all thy faithful ones and walk before thee in the land of life. 'And continually...'

3

May a good remembrance be of him before his Creator, so that he grant him to inherit of the treasure of his Maker, and that he cause his light to be bright; in fulfilment of the vision, and the prophetic word: 'For my covenant was with him, the light and the peace' and may his soul rest in the bond of life. 'And continually...'

4

The gates of heaven mayest thou find opened, and the town of peace mayest thou see, and the dwellings of confidence, and angels of peace to meet thee with joy; and may the High Priest stand to receive thee; and thou, go thou to the end, for thou shalt rest and rise up again. 'And continually...'

5

May thy soul go to the cave of Macpela, and thence to the Cherubim, may God guide it, and there may it receive a permit to the road of Paradise, and there mayest thou see a pillar leading upwards through which thou mayest ascend to heaven and not stay without; and thou, go thou to the end, for thou shalt rest and rise up again. 'And continually...'

6

The gates of the sanctuary may Michael open, and bring thy soul as an offering before God; and may the redeeming angel accompany thee unto the gates of the Heavens, where Israel dwell; may it be vouchsafed to thee to stand in this beautiful place; and thou, go thou to the end, for thou shalt rest and rise up again. 'And continually...'

7

May thy soul be bound up in the bond of life, with the Heads of the Colleges, and the Heads of the Captivity; with Israelites, Priests and Levites, and with the seven bands of just and pious men; and in Paradise thou shalt rest, and rise up again; and thou, go thou to the end, for thou shalt rest and rise up again. 'And continually . . .'

I think that the Christian burial service could be improved by prayers of this character, although the language could be less verbose and the contents would have to be amended. Sometimes the *Nunc Dimittis* is said or sung as the coffin leaves the Church; but the nearest that the Book of Common Prayer comes to the Prayer of the Seven Circuits is its beautiful commendatory prayer on a deathbed:

Go forth upon thy journey from this world, O Christian soul,
In the name of God the Father Almighty who created thee.
Amen.
In the name of Jesus Christ who suffered for thee. Amen.
In the name of the Holy Ghost who strengtheneth thee. Amen.
In communion with the blessed Saints, and aided by Angels and
Archangels, and all the armies of the heavenly host. Amen.
May thy portion this day be in peace, and thy dwelling in the
heavenly Jerusalem. Amen.

The Marriage Service

Before a Jewish wedding there is a cheerful buzz of conversation among members of the congregation who move about to greet one another, rather than the assembly sitting in solemn silence before the entry of the bride, which is more characteristic of Anglican weddings. I always used to feel that the Jewish service was gravely deficient, because the bride remains totally silent through-out. I discovered only lately that in fact she does give her consent to the marriage at the signing of the marriage contract which has to take place before the ceremony can begin. The couple to be married stand under the *Hoopah* or canopy, which I have always supposed to represent the tent of the desert, but it may have some other significance. The bridegroom breaks a glass with his foot (allegedly symbolic of the destruction of the Temple), and as he places the ring upon the finger of the bride, says: 'Behold, thou art wedded to me by this ring, according to the law of Moses and Israel.' There the follows the Seven Blessings of the Bride and Bridegroom, which introduces a particularly joyful note into the occasion. Although the translation from the Hebrew is not particularly felicitous as given in the Sephardi Prayer Book, I append it here:

Blessed art thou, O Lord, King of the universe; who hast created everything to thy glory.

Blessed art thou, O Lord, King of the universe; the Creator of man.

Blessed art thou, O Lord, King of the universe; who hast formed man in thine own image; in the image of the likeness of thy form, and hast prepared out of him an everlasting establishment.

Blessed art thou, O Lord, King of the universe, the Creator of man. She who was barren shall surely rejoice and be glad, at the gathering of her children unto her speedily.

Blessed art thou, O Lord! who causest Zion to rejoice through her children. May this loving couple delight in the joy thou didst cause thy creation of old in the Garden of Eden.

Blessed art thou, O Lord, who causest the bridegroom and bride to rejoice.

Blessed art thou, O Lord, King of the universe; who hast created joy and gladness, bridegroom and bride, love and fraternity, delight and pleasure, peace and fellowship; grant speedily, O Lord our God! that there be heard in the cities of Judah, and in the streets of Jerusalem, the voice of joy and gladness: the voice of the bridegroom and the bride; the voice of jubilant bridegrooms at their nuptial feasts, and of youths at musical entertainments.

Blessed art thou O Lord, who causest the bridegroom to rejoice with the bride and who wilt make them prosper. 'O give thanks unto the Lord, for he is good, and his mercy endureth for ever.' May joys increase in Israel, and sighs flee away.

* * *

This prayer once again shows the conservative nature of liturgy; for nowadays in the State of Israel there *is* heard in the cities of Judah and in the city of Jerusalem the voice of the bridegroom and the bride; but once a prayer has become fixed in form, it is not always easy to get it changed in orthodox liturgies.

It so happened that my wife used to be a member of the Church of England's Liturgical Commission, and the Marriage Service was coming up for revision. We both thought that some elements of the Seven Blessings, suitably transmuted into a Christian idiom, would improve the Anglican wedding service; and we together devised a 'Christian Seven Blessings'. Alas, all suggestions were subject to an enormous amount of sifting. First, the Liturgical Commission had to consider and draft a service, and then it was subject to revision by the whole Church of England's General Synod consisting of hundreds of people, before it could be finally approved. (A somewhat less cumbrous method of procedure has since been adopted.) What emerged from all this was a somewhat tame and feeble series of versicles and responses:

> Blessed are you, heavenly Father;
> You give joy to bridegroom and bride.
>
> Blessed are you, Lord Jesus Christ;
> You have brought new life to mankind.
>
> Blessed are you, Holy Spirit of God;
> You bring us together in love.
>
> Blessed be Father, Son and Holy Spirit:
> One God, to be praised for ever. Amen.

It seems to me a pity that a simple thanksgiving to God for the joy of marriage has been turned into what is essentially a Trinitarian ascription of praise; but not all battles can be fully won, and at least some note of joy has been introduced into the Marriage Service of the Alternative Services Book, derived from the Jewish Wedding Service.

Borrowings and similarities

Hymns are used in Jewish liturgy just as they are in Christian worship, although there are less of them, probably because there is not so much need of them as the service as a whole is chanted. A much loved hymn in the Jewish morning service is the *Ain kelorhainu* . . . (There is none like our God), the lines of which rhyme, all ending in *ainu*. Another much loved hymn, chanted by the congregation at the end of Morning Prayer, is the *'adon 'olam* . . . This sounds better, as so often, in the original Hebrew than in English translation:

> Lord over all! Whose power the sceptre swayed,
> Ere first creation's wondrous form was framed,
> When by his will Divine all things were made;
> Then King, Almighty, was his name proclaimed . . . etc.

Some English hymns are versions of Hebrew Psalms. One hymn which appears in Christian hymn books is a Christianised version of the Hebrew *Yigdal*:

> The God of Abraham praise
> Who reigns enthroned above,
> Ancient of everlasting Days,
> And God of love;
> Jehovah, great I AM,
> By earth and heaven confest;
> We bow and bless the sacred name
> For ever blest . . .

There are also echoes of Hebrew liturgies in some Christian rites. 'O Lord, open thou our lips; and our mouth shall proclaim thy praise' is best known from Anglican Morning and Evening service; but this verse from the Psalms also appears in the ancient Jewish prayer *Amidah*. In the same Jewish prayer there also appears this phrase, again somewhat infelicitously rendered into English:

* * *

We will sanctify and reverence thee with the harmonious utterance of the assembly of the holy Seraphim, who thrice repeat a holy phrase unto thee; for thus it is written by the hand of the prophet: 'And one cried unto the other and said [congregation]: Holy, holy, holy is the Lord of hosts! The whole earth is full of his glory.'

This is reminiscent to Christians of the Sanctus in the service of Holy Communion. I think it would surely to be agreed that, in comparison with the English translation in the Sephardi Prayer Book, Cranmer's version is greatly preferable:

Therefore with angels and archangels and with all the company of heaven, we laud and magnify thy holy name, evermore praising thee and saying: Holy, holy, holy Lord God of hosts! Heaven and earth are full of thy glory! Glory be to thee, O Lord most high!

Another ancient, well-known and much loved Jewish prayer in the liturgy is the 'alenu prayer, which begins (in English translation): 'It is our duty to praise the Lord of all; to ascribe greatness to him who formed the world in the beginning . . .' Can this be the origin of the prayer in the Christian service of Holy Communion which runs: 'It is very meet right and our bounden duty that we should at all times and in all places give thanks unto thee . . .'? The two prayers begin in a very similar manner.

Summary

Dr Oesterley has noted that 'the language of some of the prayers in the Jewish liturgy will appear as somewhat unrestrained at times; too emotional, possibly in some cases wanting in dignity, here and there almost bordering on familiarity. There is in some prayers the piling up of epithets which unnecessarily increases the length of a prayer.' But he also noted

* * *

the extraordinary intimacy assumed to exist between God and his worshippers by these prayers . . . These prayers proclaim a realization of the power and love of God, and of truthfulness and dependence upon Him on the part of man, that is extraordinarily impressive and helps one to understand how it is that Judaism has played the part it has in the dissemination of the knowledge of God in the history of the world. The wording of the prayers tell us of the *experience of God*, of an inner witness; and no one who utters them in sincerity can do so without the conviction that God is very near him. (Oesterley, 1939)

Enough of Jewish liturgies. I do in fact love our Anglican liturgies, both Cranmer's sonorous prose and balanced cadences, and the more modern and succinct approach of the Alternative Service Book. Of course I have an affection for many of the prayers in the Sephardi Prayer Book, but that in no way diminishes my love of Anglican liturgy. I speak of Anglicanism, because it is within this tradition that I am accustomed to worship, and I am not really conversant with other Christian forms of worship. But, as will have become obvious from my comparisons in this chapter, I do think there are ways in which our Christian liturgies could usefully borrow from Jewish styles and forms of prayer. This is despite the many dissimilarities between Orthodox Jewish liturgies and Christian services. In particular, the references to the Temple in Jewish liturgies have, of course, no counterpart in Christian worship.

The yawning divide is over the Messiah. The most that can be found in Jewish prayers is that he will come speedily, and even that will not be found in Liberal Jewish rites. As for Christian worship, although prayer is offered to the Father in the Spirit through the Son, liturgies tend to be rather Christocentric. It may seem that Jewish worship is rather inward looking, and that most intercession is for the Jewish people; but then it should be remembered that most prayers in the Christian prayer book are for the Church and its members. Furthermore, there are many references in Jewish worship to the fact that God has chosen the Jewish race as his own people. In Christian worship the idea of vocation is also there, but of course it refers not to the Jews but to the Church.

8

Convergences in ethics

Common principles

Jewish and Christian ethics have a great deal in common, which is
only natural as Christianity started as a sect within Judaism. When
Jesus was asked what was the greatest commandment, he is reported
to have quoted two texts from the Old Testament, Deuteronomy
6:5 and Leviticus 19:19: 'Thou shalt love the Lord thy God with all
thy heart and with all thy soul and with all thy mind' and 'Thou
shalt love thy neighbour as thyself'. Rabbi Akibah (*ob.* AD 132) also
taught that the commandment from Leviticus is 'a fundamental
principle of the Torah'. The combination of the two commandments
is found elsewhere in Jewish literature of the New Testament period.
Again, Jesus is reported to have said 'all things whatsoever ye would
that men should do unto you, do ye even so unto them: for this is
the law and the prophets.' Similarly, Rabbi Hillel (*ob. c.* 10 BC) in
answering the request of a pagan who wished to be converted to
Judaism on condition that he was taught the whole Torah while
standing on one foot, replied: 'What is hateful to yourself, do not
do to your fellow-man' (Shab. 31a). Jesus, when confronted by a
young man who had asked him what he should do to inherit eternal
life, replied by asking him whether he had kept the Ten
Commandments.

It is hardly surprising that since Jesus was a Jew he took

commandments from the Torah. In the light of this it is even less surprising that there is a striking convergence between Jewish and Christian ethics. 'Down to approximately 250 CE Christian ethics were in the main Judaic' (Snape, 1938). Hans Küng, reflecting on the urgent need for a contemporary ethic that could unite all humankind, commented: 'A common ethic does not need to be invented but it is already deeply rooted in the religious traditions; in the Ten Commandments of the Hebrew Bible and in key texts of the New Testament and of the Qu'ran' (Küng, 1992). So far as ethics are concerned, there is little difficulty for a Jewish Christian in any attempt to live as a Christian and as a loyal Jew.

Both Jewish and Christian ethics take their start from belief in God. The moral imperative in both religions is obedience to God who is both righteous and loving. Both religions are forms of ethical monotheism. Not all forms of monotheism are ethical and not all systems of ethics are rooted in theistic belief. 'It is only when the Deity is conceived monotheistically and as transcendent moral perfection that religion can profoundly influence ethics' (Elmslie, 1938). Again, belief in the dignity of human beings both in Judaism and in Christianity is based on the common assumption that all men and women are created in the image of God (Gen. 1:27), and so all must be treated with respect.

It is common to both faiths that a righteous God demands righteous dealing between members of the human race. We associate this demand for justice particularly with the canonical prophets, but it is also found strongly in other parts of the Hebrew Scriptures, such as the Torah and in the Wisdom Literature. Nor must justice be understood as merely giving every man and woman their due. 'What does the Lord require of thee' asks the prophet Micah, 'but to do justly and to love mercy and to walk humbly with thy God?' (Mic. 6:8) Much more than bare justice is required. The impoverished, the widow and the orphan are to receive ungrudging aid, not as a charity, but as justice due to them; and similarly kindness must be shown to debtors and to others in distress. These same ethical imperatives are to be found in the New Testament, derived from the tradition enshrined in the Hebrew Scriptures.

Convergences in ethics

Some differences

Despite these striking convergences, it is only natural that over the centuries the two traditions should have diverged on details, even if they are agreed on fundamentals. For example a distinction that must be made between Christian and Jewish ethics is that Christians are enjoined to act 'in Christ', as members of his body the Church, acting in his Spirit and in his power. Jews, with their belief in direct access to God, naturally have nothing corresponding to this.

Again, there is emphasised in the New Testament the Christian duty of *mimesis*. Christians are enjoined to imitate Jesus, not of course in his actions, in so far as we know them, but in his attitudes. 'Follow me' wrote St Paul, 'as I follow Christ'. I do not think that Jewish ethics has anything corresponding to this kind of *mimesis*, with the exception of the biblical injunction 'Be holy as I am holy'. The imitation of God does not play such a key part in Jewish ethics. But holiness does. Holiness in Leviticus 19 means moral purity and moral righteousness. God is holy because he is essentially loving and good. Claude Montefiore analysed moral holiness according to Jewish criteria as follows:

1. Reverence of parents.
2. Charity to the poor.
3. Truth of word and deed.
4. Justice in all business transactions.
5. Honour shown to the aged.
6. Equal justice to the poor to rich and poor.
7. No talebearing or malice.
8. The love of one's neighbour.
9. The love of the resident alien. (Montefiore, 1927)

A further difference between Jewish and Christian ethics lies in the Jewish observance of the Torah, the Law contained in the first five books of the Bible. This Law contains both ritual and moral laws, although I don't think that the orthodox Jew would make that kind of distinction: the Law is the Law and should be obeyed. The

Pentateuch, or first five books of the Bible, contains 248 positive injunctions and 365 prohibitions.

The Law of Moses has to be interpreted, and the Mishnah and the Talmud contain interpretations; and further interpretation that is needed today is given by a rabbi (that is his primary job, not to be a pastor but to interpret the Law of Moses). It is often said by Christians that the meticulous observance of the Law by Jews leads to legalism, an accusation (and it must be said, a caricature) which is sometimes found in the New Testament. Doubtless some Jews were legalists (as are some Christians), but Christians usually do not understand that when the Law is observed meticulously by Jews this is not so much legalism as sheer delight, delight on the part of Jews in the meticulous doing of God's will and in sanctifying his name by so doing. *Kiddush Hashem*, sanctification of his Name, has been recognised as the most characteristic feature of Jewish ethics, both as principle and as motive (Epstein, 1959). Such a principle is a hundred miles from legalism. By contrast, the deciding of moral issues in accordance with the Code of Canon Law, as happens within the Roman Catholic Church, might well seem a Christian form of legalism.

Meticulous observance of the Jewish law in the Scriptures can occasionally lead to unfortunate results, and it is partly for this reason that Jews of the Reform have broken away from the literal application of the Jewish Torah in all its particulars. Even the conservative Rabbi Louis Jacobs has written that 'where the *Halachah* [teaching] as it is presently practised results in the kind of injustice that reasonable people could see as detrimental to Judaism itself, a frank avowal is called for that there must be a change in the law'. Rabbi Jacobs was writing about the *Manserim*. the children of incest or adultery. According to Jewish law, they and their children may marry other *Manserim* and no one else for up to ten generations. Lists of such people are kept among the Orthodox in Jerusalem, who refuse to alter the law. It must be remembered however that it is not long since illegitimates were also disadvantaged under Christian law. I myself can remember, when I was teaching at an Anglican seminary, an occasion when a student, born illegitimate, had to have a special 'faculty' before he could be ordained. Thankfully this has now changed.

It is sometimes said that divergences between Jewish and Christian ethics emerge mostly clearly in the antitheses found in the Sermon on the Mount in St Matthew's Gospel: 'It was said of old time . . . But I say unto you . . .' However these passages need to be considered in more detail before such a judgment can be accepted.

It is true that such extreme commands as 'Resist not evil', or 'Give to him that asketh' or 'Love your enemies' are not found as such in rabbinic writings. But similar sentiments are found tempered with common sense. Jews were ordered to love their neighbours, and the alien who lived nearby, and it is among these that their enemies were to be found. The duty of almsgiving to those in need is constantly stressed by the rabbis. Christian writers, when commenting on Jewish moral teaching, seldom pick out the high spots, but rather concentrate on less exalted moral teaching; but when they write about Jesus's teaching, it is usually judged by the tenets of the Sermon on the Mount rather than his tirades against the scribes and the Pharisees. (The depiction of the Pharisees in the Gospels is grotesque, and I like to think these tirades represent later quarrels between them and Jewish Christians rather than the words of Jesus himself.) I don't believe that the teaching of Jesus is any more universalistic than that of the rabbis. For example Hillel said: 'Love peace and pursue peace; love thy fellow creatures and draw them near to the Torah.' That is as universalist as anything in the Gospels. It is sometimes said that rabbinic exhortation to well doing is based on prudential motives, in that such conduct will ultimately benefit those who do well. Again, some of Jesus's teaching is not wholly different, promising happiness and eternal life to those who act thus.

Criticism of Jesus's ethics

Jews have criticised the moral teaching of Jesus in that it is unattainable; and certainly the track record of Christianity hardly bears witness to constant love of one's foes, or going the extra mile, or not resisting one's enemies. Rabbinic teaching, they claim, is more down to earth, more practical, more within a person's grasp. That is true; but at the same time the idealism of Jesus is needed as much as the practical injunctions of the rabbis. Here at the risk of a long quotation, I must cite my cousin Claude Montefiore at some length, because I think that, writing as a Jew, he puts both points of view so fairly:

> The Jewish writers have to be criticised as well. They exalt the Old Testament and the Talmud too much. For these documents, like the Gospels, have their moral inadequacies as well as their moral excellencies, and these are not to be avoided or evaded. Of these inadequacies, the hatred of national enemies, the ascription of hatred to God of Israel's foes, the hatred of the internal heretic and sometimes even of the opposite party, are conspicuous. Secondly, the injunction 'Love your enemies', sensibly interpreted, is a noble and inspiring ideal. The usual Jewish criticism of 'Love your enemies' is that it is paradoxical, impracticable and absurd. One seldom opens a Jewish book or pamphlet which deals with Jesus and the New Testament without finding this criticism . . .
>
> It is in fact contended by Jewish critics that the defect in the ethical teaching of Jesus is that it strung so high that it has failed to produce solid and practical results just where its admirers vaunt that it differs from, and is superior to, the ethical codes of the Pentateuch, the Prophets and the Rabbis. The old codes said: 'Bear no grudge'; 'do not revenge'; if your enemy is in distress and you can help him, do so. The Jewish critics contend that human nature *can* go as far as this, and that if you so order and urge men, they will not wholly and markedly fail; whereas if you go further, and say '*Love* your enemies', you ask what cannot be given. Hence your command is neglected, and the result of this unpractical injunction is that things are worse than they were. The bow is so bent that it cracks altogether. The history of Christianity is, so the Jewish critics say, a proof that their criticism

of Jesus's teaching is accurate . . . Thus upon the side of public enemies and the enemies of religion, Christians, with their brand new command 'Love your enemies' have hated their enemies and persecuted them quite as much as could have conceivably happened under the 'dispensation' of Pentateuch, Prophets and Rabbis, while upon the side of private enemies, there is no reason whatever to believe that Jews have not acted up to as high an ethical standard as Christians . . .

Does this criticism miss the point? It largely does so . . . Jesus can hardly have meant that we ought to have the same emotional feelings of affection for the 'enemy' as for a bosom friend . . . He idealises; he is filled with enthusiasm. He generalises, and he rivets attention by his brief fine generalisation. He means that active and helpful love must have no limits. Above all it must have nothing to do with requital and tit for tat. It must look for no reward except from God. We are to wish no man evil, and (so far as in us lies) to do all men good. This is the meaning of the word 'love'. We must never avoid the chance of doing a good turn to the man who hates us and has done us an evil turn. We must rather even seek out the chance for good, and conquer hatred by love. Thus interpreted, his teaching, though it may soar higher, and strike a more passionate and fuller note, seems to be in accordance with those best sayings of the Rabbis which Jewish apologists are never weary of quoting again and again. The main difference is that the injunctions of Jesus (even as traditionally reported) are given in a form which, in every language and translation, arrests attention, and stimulates the heart and the mind in the highest degree possible.

Christian and Jewish ethical principles

Christian ethics have developed out of the teaching of Jesus. The teaching of the Church on moral issues has been based on a combination of sources; the teaching of Jesus, the so-called natural law, scriptural teaching, the tradition of the Church and moral reasoning. Evangelicals have tended to rest their ethics on those of the New Testament and to have left it to one's private judgment to apply these to the issues of everyday life. There was for a time a fashion in Christian ethics for so called 'situation ethics', which does away with objective morality altogether, and leaves it to the individual person to make the most loving response in each situation without applying any objective principle. This is not satisfactory: we need moral norms of behaviour even if these cannot always be applied to each and every situation.

Catholic theology has tended to make use of purely objective norms, and has used various systems for so doing. For example the system of probabalism holds that any option that can be proved, that is to say, that can be morally justified, can be acceptable. Probabiliorism holds that the option which is more likely to be morally justified should be chosen, while tutiorism holds that the safest option should always be chosen. Jewish teaching does not deal in this kind of casuistry. There is nothing systematic about Jewish ethics or theology. Allegory could be used in the interpretation of biblical texts to achieve a conclusion that probably was originally derived from intuition. None the less the principle of tutiorism was often employed, although unacknowledged as such. A fence was put round the law to prevent accidental breaches. Thus rules for keeping the Sabbath were based on the 'safest' definition of work, which according to the Scriptures is forbidden on the Sabbath. As we have noticed earlier, the biblical command 'Thou shalt not seethe a kid in its mother's milk' gave rise for the prohibition of combining milk and meat. Milk products, according to strict orthodoxy, may only be eaten up to an hour before meat is consumed. This is because the milk might come from the mother of the animal whose meat is being consumed: both might meet in the stomach of the consumer, and thus the Law of Moses would be breached. The odds in favour of this happening may be minimal: nevertheless is *might* happen, and the principle of tutiorism should prevail, and a fence was therefore placed around the Law. Another principle of rabbinic ethics in adapting biblical commands to contemporary usage is the *a fortiori* argument, known as *kal vahomer*, 'If this, how much more that'. This kind of argumentation is acceptable to Orthodox Jews.

Those who are progressives, and who belong to the Reform or Liberal congregations, do not regard themselves bound by all the ritual and other commandments of the Scriptures, although they respect most of the moral laws found in them. Thus a woman who belongs to these movements would take seriously the commandments about almsgiving, but would feel free to ignore the *mikveh* or ritual bath which a woman should take at the end of her menstrual period, before she is 'fit' for her husband.

Much of Jewish ethics is based on fundamental human rights. Foremost, there is the right to life, which includes also a right to be protected from a threat to life and limb. A man is under an obligation to come to the rescue of anyone whose life is under threat. Associated with the right to life is the right to possess the means of a livelihood. Under this heading, unfair means of preventing competition, graft and sleaze associated with business are all condemned. Equally forbidden are all kinds of dishonesty in commerce and trade. In the same way, a labourer has rights to a just wage which may not be arbitrarily changed in a way that diminishes a man's standard of living.

Another human right is that of the human person. Even 'the dust of slander' is forbidden in rabbinic ethics, together with anything that diminishes a person's self-respect. For the same reason deception and lies are equally forbidden. Hatred is wrong, and so is even the harbouring of a grudge. Human liberty is an inalienable right of the human person. The principle of equality gave rise to complex laws relating to the relations of slave and master.

The right of the human person requires relief to be given to the poor (Lev. 25:35). Right to life includes the right to clothing and shelter. Almsgiving had great importance in rabbinic Judaism. *Zedakah*, the Hebrew word for righteousness, came to mean any charity devoted to the relief of the poor.

In the Scriptures interest on a loan was forbidden between Jews (although it was permitted in the case of a non-Jew, which enabled Christians to force Jews into moneylending). Ingenious ways of circumventing this law, known as 'the dust of interest', were also forbidden. Then in the post-rabbinic period circumstances changed; and the exigencies of trade resulted in further ways of circumventing the law. You could get your friend to act as an agent in arranging interest-bearing loans: the law only forbade transactions directly between borrower and lender. Nowadays interest is generally allowed. In the Christian tradition, all interest was once forbidden, but with the rise of capitalism, and with money lent not against poverty but for investment, the situation became impossible. The Roman Catholic Church made a *volte-face*. The prohibition was never repealed: it was relegated to the lumber room, and usury was permitted. Calvin distinguished between money lent against a person's need and investment to create wealth: the latter was permitted. Now all loans may be interest-bearing, but when we think of Third-World debt, it is clear that, contrary to the Hebrew Scriptures, interest is now charged against desperate need.

Sex

On the subject of sex there is – or there was – a considerable difference of outlook between Christians and Jews. In the Roman Catholic Church until the Second Vatican Council this century, sexual intercourse was regarded as purely for the procreation of the children. The pleasures of sex were regarded as a somewhat dubious male indulgence which was an inevitable accompaniment of the act of procreation. The Second Vatican Council, however, asserted that the mutual love of husband and wife was as important as the procreation of children. In the Church of England the Book of Common Prayer gave 'the mutual society help and comfort which the one ought to have of the other' as only the third reason for marriage, the first two being the procreation of children and a remedy against fornication. In the 1928 Prayer Book, marriage was declared to be 'in order that the natural instincts and affections, implanted by God, should be hallowed and directed aright' (in place of a remedy against fornication), while in the Alternative Service Book 1980 it is asserted that marriage 'is given that with delight and tenderness they may know each other in love, and through the joy of their bodily union, may strengthen the union of their hearts and lives'. A more positive view of sex within marriage has made its appearance in Christian liturgies this century, thus reversing a centuries-old tradition of playing down sex and regarding it as a somewhat ambiguous accompaniment of procreation and conception.

The Jewish attitude towards marriage has always been more earthy.

> Sexual shame is foreign to Jews. In our tradition, a man is supposed to make love to his wife on the sabbath, because it is a form of joy and one should rejoice on the sabbath. When the sixteenth century mystics were proclaiming 'Come, my beloved, to greet the bride' that wonderful song by Solomon Alkabetz to welcome the sabbath bride, they were referring to the sabbath perceived as a female entity. The imagery of the sexual joy of the sabbath should not be lost on anyone. Sexual delight is part of what the sabbath is all about. (Neuberger, 1996)

I can't in my wildest dreams imagine any Christian saying that about Sunday! Nor can I imagine a woman asking a divorce court to press her husband for divorce on the grounds that he cannot give her sexual satisfaction. (Women cannot actually sue for divorce under Jewish law.) A woman is entitled to sexual satisfaction as much as her husband according to Jewish tradition (Exod. 21:10), while in Christian thinking it is only in this century that such an idea has been entertained.

As for contraception, the Rabbis, according to the Talmud, permitted the use of the *mokh* (a kind of contraceptive barrier) to three categories of women; a minor, a pregnant woman and a nursing mother. Of course progressive Jews do not keep to these regulations, any more than members of reformed churches. Roman Catholics, as is well known, are not supposed to use any form of artificial contraception. We find here the same kind of divisions between orthodox and reformed in both faiths. The same applies to lesbianism and homosexuality, which is tolerated in reformed churches, but forbidden to Roman Catholics. These are regarded as abominations in the Torah, and therefore prohibited to Orthodox Jews. Progressive Jews however are not required to keep these prohibitions. The present Chief Rabbi of the United (Orthodox) Synagogue made himself very unpopular with some sections of British Jewry when he refused to permit the Jewish Gay Group to join in a procession in Hyde Park in 1992.

Divorce, it is well known, is not permitted to Roman Catholics (although marriages may in certain circumstances be regarded as null and void). The Church of England is somewhat ambivalent on the subject. However there is no stigma over divorce among Jews, and an Orthodox Jew is required to divorce his wife if no children have appeared after ten years, because of the biblical injunction to 'be fruitful and multiply'. A divorced woman is expected to remarry. During the New Testament period there were disputes over divorce between the two schools of Hillel and Shammai, Hillel taking the more lenient view that a man could divorce his wife for reasons which seem trivial today, while Shammai took a stronger line. In fact Jewish marriages break down for the same reasons as Christian marriages, and there is little difference between the two Faiths in this. Feminism comes up against similar obstacles in both Faiths, since in both Judaism and Christianity God is depicted predominantly in male imagery, and both Faiths (in their orthodox forms) are patriarchal in outlook. Women do not have equal status, although the situation is changing in progressive Judaism and reformed Christianity, aided and abetted by ordination of women to the Christian priesthood, and by the ordination of women as rabbis.

As for abortion, the foetus in the Hebrew Scriptures is regarded as not yet a human person, as can be seen from the stipulations in Exodus 21:22 with its differing penalties for the manslaughter of a pregnant woman and for hurting her in such a way that she has a miscarriage.

Most rabbinic authorities do not permit abortion unless the mother's life is in danger, but a few permit it in cases of extreme mental anguish, and one, Rabbi Jacob Emdon, who lived in the eighteenth century, allowed it for reasons of extreme shame, as when a young woman has become pregnant adulterously and is now contrite. (Neuberger, 1996)

(However a child that dies within thirty days of birth is not allowed by the Orthodox a service of burial or a *Kaddish*.) Within the Christian Church abortion is absolutely forbidden in the Roman Catholic Church. In the Church of England there are divisions on the matter. Some are absolutely against it, while others agree to it under certain conditions. Almost all would agree that the present abortion law, which permits abortion almost on demand, is an intolerable scandal

Social ethics

The Chief Rabbi today is one of the foremost exponents of social ethics in the country. There is a good reason for this. Judaism has in its foundation documents a considerable body of what may be called social ethics, because ancient Israel was not exactly a theocracy, but it formed a society where the whole people was subject to the rule of God. By contrast Christianity started as a sect within Judaism, and until it was established as the official religion of the Roman Empire under Constantine the Great, it was not the religion of a region. There were plenty of exhortations about how people should behave towards one another within the Church, but not about social ethics. The Church developed such thinking much later. It was derived for the most part not from the Scriptures but from the application of the natural law. There is to be found in the Roman Catholic Church a whole series of encyclicals on social ethics, beginning in the last century. Other church traditions have also developed their own social ethics, although not so systematically and not in such an authoritative fashion, so that differences may be found between different writers. Some, alas, have tried to adapt the principles of the Sermon on the Mount, which was addressed to individuals, and have applied them simplistically to relations between countries. I suppose that pacifism, a minority view within

Christendom is an example of this. It hardly exists at all within Israel. It calls itself a secular State, and it makes little attempt to keep strictly to social ethics derived from biblical and talmudic sources. At the same time it must be said that in so-called Christian countries there have been gross and continuing breaches of Christian social ethics.

A personal summary

Although there are differences, as we have seen, between Christian and Jewish ethical traditions, the convergencies are far greater than the divergences. Judaism is primarily a religion of orthopraxy rather than orthodoxy, and so ethical issues have been and are of greater importance. By contrast Christianity, despite some internal disagreement over particular ethical issues, has paid more attention to matters of Christian doctrine. For a Jew who becomes a Christian, there is a clear change of emphasis here.

At the same time I have not been conscious of many different demands upon my moral behaviour on joining the Christian Church, other than loyalty and fellowship within the Christian congregation to which I have happened to belong. It is the same moral God who is worshipped in both Faiths, and who demands moral behaviour. Righteousness and truth belong to him, and righteousness and truth is demanded of Christian and Jew alike. I think that the moral absolutism of the teaching of Jesus, as portrayed in the Sermon on the Mount, has enthused and inspired me in a way which was formerly lacking, and in trying to do God's will I have been conscious of the grace of God in my life and of the inspiration of the Holy Spirit; but these two latter influences are not peculiar to Christianity. Again, I think that the love of God has been made clearer to me through Jesus Christ who is for me transparent to God; but at the same time I was conscious of that love in Judaism, and of the requirement that I return that love to God and show it my fellow human beings. I think that I have been influenced by the Enlightenment both before and after my conversion. It seems to me pre-eminently necessary to apply reason to revelation, whether this be revealed doctrine or revealed ethics. It is clear to me that the Enlightenment has influenced progressive Judaism as much as it has influenced liberal Catholicism and liberal Protestantism.

Above all I am conscious of falling short over and over again in carrying out the ethical teaching both of Judaism and of Christianity, and I am aware of the graciousness of God who enables us to pick ourselves up and to start all over again.

9

Jewish Christians

Are there many Jewish Christians? They don't seem very evident. But there are many more than people think, certainly more than most Gentile Christians suppose.

> The vast majority of Christians think that it is virtually a miracle if a Jew comes to faith in Christ, and that the Church's approach to the Jew is at best a magnificent gesture. When we tell them that *proportionately* the Church's proclamation to the Jew in the nineteenth and twentieth centuries has been *at least* as successful as its proclamation on the ordinary mission field, and indeed much more successful than in some, we are met with polite incredulity. Yet so far as the nineteenth century is concerned, the statement is confirmed by serious works of research. (Ellison, 1954)

As we have seen, the Gentile Church of the period which followed the Council of Nicaea in AD 325 put an end to Jewish Christianity. So Jews who have become Christians have been, until recently, all swallowed up in the overwhelmingly Gentile Church. Professor Dalman has been quoted as saying: 'If all Jews who have embraced Christianity had remained a distinct people instead of being absorbed by the nations among whom they dwelt, their descendants would be counted in millions.'

Why have these Jews become Christians? No doubt their full motives are hidden to us, and possibly also to themselves. The vast majority of Jewish Christians have, I am sure, been baptised for reasons of spiritual conviction, believing that God has called them to follow Christ, and convinced from the Scriptures that Christ is indeed the Messiah. But it has to be admitted that a good number have in the past been forced to the font by Christians. Although the Church has always officially frowned on forcible baptisms, these have taken place; and, according to the Roman Catholic Church's doctrine of *opus operatum*, once baptism has been administered a person has become a Christian and must be brought up as a Christian. Others, in particular many Marrano Jews of Spain, have become Christians in order to avoid persecution and even death, although many of them continued secretly to practice Jewish rites and customs until they were smoked out by the Inquisition. This has applied to past members of my own mother's family, the de Passes, in Spain.

Some in the past have found that baptism is the way into civilised society. An attempt has been made even to justify this.

> Beginning with the last century and the rise of liberalism, a large number of Jews assimilated into western culture accepted baptism and the creed of the Christian church simply, to use the words of Heinrich Heine, as an entrance ticket to modern society. If religious faith, whether Jewish or Christian, really failed to mean anything to these men, then I find nothing reprehensible in their attitude and the step they took, seeing that western society did demand an external profession of Christianity as a label of respectability. (Baum, 1960)

Personally I find it difficult to go along with this judgment. It suggests a lack of integrity.

A few Jews in the past may have taken the step of baptism not only for the sake of 'respectability' but also for financial gain. For example, in Prussia a Jew was offered the bonus of ten ducats at his baptism by Frederick William III, and Frederick William IV offered a wedding present to every baptised Jewess at her wedding! (Jocz, 1949).

It is such people who have earned the contempt of their fellow-Jews. At the same time it should be realised that there were Jewish Christians who found themselves in great financial difficulties as a result of their baptism. In the Middle Ages, since the possessions of Jews were the personal property of the king, these passed to him at their baptism and they were left penniless. Henry III founded in what has now become Chancery Lane in London a *domus conversorum*, that is to say a kind of almshouse where converted Jews might live; and similar houses were opened in Southwark and Oxford. In the last century in Germany the situation of converts became difficult. 'Many of these were wandering about, with their baptismal certificates in their hands as evidence of their "conversion", begging' (Jocz, 1949). Such is the solidarity of Jewish communities that severance from them spelt penury; and Christians tended to stand aloof. Here in England the London Jews Society was formed in the last century to provide shelter and employment. The money spent trying to help these converts gave rise to the taunt that it cost £600 to make a single Jewish convert! One charitable society even purchased land in Palestine to settle such convert families.

There have also been a good many Jews who have become Christian in heart but who have not taken the step of baptism out of loyalty to their race and to their families. This is especially understandable when one considers the history of Jews at the hands of Christians. Jewish communities had to be close-knit and Jewish families had to develop strong bonds. The philosopher Henri Bergson, for example, made it clear in his will that he had felt unable to ask for baptism at a time when anti-Semitism was growing. He was not alone. The pressures on those who did convert could be very great. It is noteworthy that the son of the Zionist leader Theodor Herzl committed suicide after he had become a Roman Catholic.

Occasionally Jewish Christians seem ashamed of their Jewish roots. (I know one bishop in the Church of England who has never admitted them.) The vast majority of Jews who have become Christians have simply been absorbed into the predominantly

Gentile churches, and even if some of them have retained some Jewish loyalties and love of Jewish customs and spirituality, it is very unlikely that their children will have done so. Since there is no Jewish Christian community, those children are most likely to have married Gentiles, and the grandchildren of the original convert may hardly have known that one quarter of their genetic inheritance is Jewish. Intermarriage, particularly in Germany, had been very common. A large number of Jews caught up in the Nazi persecution were found to be Christians with a half or a quarter Jewish blood, a far greater proportion than Hitler and his advisers had anticipated when they launched their anti-Jewish policies. Mixed marriages are also very common in England.

Quite apart from statesmen such as Disraeli, there have been many distinguished Jewish Christians down the centuries who have achieved eminence or who have contributed greatly to Christian learning. Such people have been the subject of historical research (Schonfield, 1936). They include Emmanuel Tremellius, who was for a time Regius Professor of the Old Testament at Cambridge and who helped to frame the Thirty-Nine Articles and the Book of Common Prayer. They also include Professor August Neander, the famous church historian. Dr Michael Salomon Alexander was the first Anglican bishop in Jerusalem (and incidentally by no means the only Jewish Christian bishop).

After Nicaea, in the Middle Ages and at the Reformation, Jews who became Christians were all swallowed up in Gentile Church. It is only in more recent times that there have been a few Jewish Christians who have adopted a more positive stance towards Judaism. The Polish Rabbi Abraham Schwarzenberg was baptised at the age of 64. He called himself 'a believing Jew'. He preached Christ to the Jews, but he still kept his beard and dressed like a Jew until he died at the age of 80 in 1842. More influential was Joseph Rabinowitsch. He had tried in vain to reform Russian Judaism, and then became a keen Zionist and emigrated to Palestine. After reading the New Testament he became convinced that Jesus was the Messiah. His was an authentic Jewish Christianity: he received no outside help from Gentile Christians. After baptism he continued

Jewish customs. He spoke Hebrew fluently and he continued to hold to circumcision and the keeping of the Sabbath. He called his Jewish community in Bessarabia 'Israelites of the New Covenant'. His influence in the Russian Empire was very great, reaching it is said even to Siberia. He met with opposition not only from Jews but also from the Russian government. But there were no followers to continue his work. His movement failed after his death.

Rabinowitsch had great influence on some Western Gentile Christians. Among them was Canon Box here in England who enthused about the possibility of a liturgy which was both Jewish and Christian. He even worked out a tentative form of Evensong to be used by Jewish Christians on Saturday evenings. What Rabinowitsch had raised was the possibility of a Jewish Christian church. But the Jewish Christian community formed by Rabinowitsch did not long outlast his lifetime. This was a situation which was not unique. Christian Theodor Lucky of Galicia was another Eastern European Jew, a man of great Talmudic learning and Christian faith, a keen missionary, who at the same time lived the life of an Orthodox Jew. He, rather like Rabinowitsch, became a leader of a movement of Christian Hasidim in Lwow and Stanislawow; but the movement disintegrated after his death. Other Jewish Christians like Rabbi Isaac Lichtenstein of Tapio-Szele in Hungary were devout believers in Jesus as Messiah, and declared this to their fellow Jews. But they did not form Jewish Christian communities.

An attempt was made in Britain to form a Jewish Christian community by Dr Paul Levertoff. His is a moving story, as told by his daughter Olga (Levertoff, 1939). Paul was born in Russia in the Hasidic Jewish tradition, and himself represented the younger generation of Jewish scholarship. In preparing for the rabbinate, he was introduced to more liberal ideas in college and after reading the New Testament became a Christian, but with a difference. 'Christianity is Judaism with its hopes fulfilled', and his lecture tours in Eastern Europe caught the imagination of young people awakening from the dreamland of the ghetto. His books outlined a distinctive Jewish Christianity, expressing Jewish aspiration and

Christian fulfilment. At the outset of the First World War he held a chair of Rabbinics in Leipsig, working on the Talmud and Jewish mysticism. After imprisonment, he came to England in 1919 where he made many friends and embraced liberal Catholicism. After a period on the staff at Hawarden, where he was ordained to the priesthood in the Church of England, he came to London, and became Vicar of Holy Trinity, Shoreditch, at that time a parish with many Jews within its boundaries. It was there that he tried to form a Jewish Christian church within the 'Church Catholic', expressing its Christian belief in Jewish forms of worship and reinterpreting Christian belief in terms which Jews could understand. He wrote (in Latin!) a service of Eucharist which he called 'The Meal of the Holy King' with music based on traditional Jewish chants. He was anxious to divorce the work he was doing, in the mind of the Jewish community, from traditional Christian missionary work. But the Jewish Christian congregation did not thrive, and in the end Holy Trinity Shoredith had to be regarded as a clearing house for experiments rather than as a centre of Jewish Christian worship.

There are those who have been enthusiastic for a Jewish Christian church.

Non-Jewish terms, associated (for the Jews) with distasteful historical recollections, constitute a very serious obstacle between Christianity and Judaism. Could they not be removed by Jewish Christians? Centuries of use have made these Greek words sacred for us, Christians of gentile descent, but there is no need to enforce them upon Jews. Why should a Jewish Christian use the word Christ (*Christos*) instead of the Hebrew Messiah – which means exactly the same – or, to revive an historical name of the Jewish Christians, 'Nazarene'? Why should he speak of the 'Church' instead of the Hebrew *qahal* or *haburah*, which stand for religious community? (Gillet, 1942)

The writer continues:

We would like to say again that we are not pleading here for any particular form of Jewish Christianity: we are merely considering possibilities. We do not know whether there will be a Jewish Christian revival, nor, if there is one, what forms it may assume. But we wish to emphasise two points. In the first place we are convinced that a Jewish Christianity, under some form, is desirable for the good of the whole Christian Church ... Secondly we believe that the development of a Jewish Christianity is inseparably linked with the development, among Christians, of a new oecumenical consciousness.

However desirable this may seem in principle, there are good reasons for failure to build up Jewish Christian congregations. They tended to depend on the leadership of one person, but they need a relationship to the whole Church of God: without this they tend to fail. Another reason is that Judaism is essentially the religion of a people, even though there may be a few proselytes and converts. Jews as a race have overwhelmingly rejected Christianity. If Jews have a religious faith, it is almost always Judaism in one shape or form. But the Church of God is essentially universal. It does not depend upon a particular nation (even though churches like the Church of England may be nationally based). It follows that a Jewish Christian church could only come into being among a Jewish Christian people. Except in a few centres of Jewish population, Jewish Christians in the Gentile world are too few and far between to form a Jewish Christian church, even if it were desirable to do so. But it not so desirable, for it would contradict the claim that Jesus Christ has (as St Paul put it) broken down the middle wall of partition that divides Jews and Gentiles. In other words, it would be a denial of that unity which lies at the heart of the Christian gospel.

The Faith and Order Commission of the World Council of Churches addressed this issue in August 1967:

Christ himself is the ground and substance of this continuity [between Israel in the Old Testament and the Church]. This is underlined by the preservation of the Old Testament in the Church as an integral part of her worship and tradition. The existence of Christians of Jewish descent provides a visible manifestation of that same continuity, though many Christians are hardly aware of this. The presence of such members in a Church which in the course of time has become composed predominantly of Gentiles, witnesses to the truthworthiness of God's promises, and should serve to remind the Church of her origins in Israel. We are not advocating separate congregations for them. History has shown the twofold danger which lies in this: the danger of discriminating despite all the intentions to the contrary, and the danger that such separate congregations tend to evolve sectarian traits. But more important than these considerations is that in Christ the dividing wall has been broken down and Jew and Gentile are to form one new man; thus any separation in the Church has become impossible.

However, without detracting in any way from what has just been said, we should remember that there is room for all kinds of peoples and cultures in the church. This implies that Jews who become Christians are not simply required to abandon their Jewish traditions and ways of thinking; in certain circumstances it may therefore be right to form special groups which are composed mainly of Jewish Christians.

This has happened in Britain. In 1866 the Hebrew Christian Alliance was formed, arising out of an earlier Hebrew Christian Association formed in Jews' Chapel, London, a half century earlier. In America a Hebrew Christian Alliance was formed in 1915, and in 1925 an International Alliance. In Britain the Alliance was first formed in order that Jewish Christians might get to know each other better and support one another. The aims of the International Alliance were formulated as follows:

1. To foster a spirit of fellowship and co-operation among Hebrew Christians thoughout the world:
    (a) by the establishment of local National Alliances wherever possible;
    (b) by watching over the spiritual development and

general welfare of Hebrew Christians and encouraging them to be witnesses for Christ among Israel in every sphere of life, and thus set up again, under Divine guidance 'the candlestick of witness within Jewry'.

2.   To present a united witness on behalf of Christ not only to the Jewish people but also to the world.

3.   To interpret the spirit of the Jewish people to the Christian world, and the spirit of the Christian Gospel to the Jews.

4.   To aid Churches and Societies in their selection of Hebrew Christian candidates for the Ministry; and to supply them with information concerning converts as occasion may arise.

5.   To identify Hebrew Christians with the Jewish people in defence of their rights in countries in which these rights are denied them, and, when necessary, to protest against the spirit of anti-Semitism.

It will be noted that these aims are somewhat evangelistic in tone, and they reflect the evangelical bias of the Alliance. Sadly it must be admitted that the aims have far from been fulfilled. If the Alliance has watched over *my* spiritual development, I have been unaware of this! I do not recall any way in which the International Alliance has been a united witness to the Jewish people or to the world. I fear it has not been successful in interpreting the spirit of the Jewish people to the Christian world, or the Spirit of the Christian Gospel to the Jews. I don't think that it has had much or anything to do with candidates for the ministry, nor do I think that its voice has been heard against the spirit of anti-Semitism.

I do not think that the Alliance should necessarily be blamed for any of these failures. Some of the objectives perhaps were misconceived, and the Alliance achieved little publicity, failing to gain the allegiance of many Jewish Christians who either have not heard of it, or who do not altogether agree with all of its aims.

Lately the Alliance has changed its name to the Alliance of

Messianic Jews. while retaining its old name in brackets. This gives the impression that being Jewish receives more emphasis than being Christian, and for that reason I have resigned from it. In any case I have not noticed in its literature much about membership of the Christian Church. The writings of the Alliance seem to me to concentrate on the Jewish Messiahship of Jesus rather than on Christ in his one, holy, catholic and apostolic Church. Their quarterly magazine seems almost entirely given over to the interpretation of Old Testament prophesy and to the testimony of Jews who have embraced Christ. Possibly this is due to its evangelical bias.

I suspect that the Hebrew Christian Alliance changed its name because of the apparent success of the 'Messianic Jews' movement in the USA, focused on the West Coast. There are some six million Jews in the USA and it is claimed that as many as three hundred thousand Jews have joined Messianic Jewish congregations, such as that of Tiferet Israel in San Francisco which describes itself as 'A Messianic Congregation of Jewish and Gentile Believers in Y'Shua the Messiah'. (Y'shua is a transliteration of the Hebrew name Joshua, *Ieseus* in the Greek New Testament and hence Jesus in English. I notice that Messianic Jews always seem to call Jesus Y'shua.) There are some hundred Messianic Jewish congregations in America, mostly formed into three main alliances. They function somewhat under the independent Baptist model, and are usually fundamentalist in tone. 'Jews for Jesus' was founded by Moishe Rosen in 1973, and he claims to have raised more than $9 million through church collections. Fundamentalist churches like the Southern Baptists back the movement, not least because they believe that the Second Advent will not come until the Jewish race has embraced the gospel, and some expect wonderful things with the coming of the Millennium.

Messianic Jews celebrate the coming of the Sabbath on Friday evenings with a service followed by a Jewish style *kiddush* of bread and wine. Some of them keep Saturday as the Sabbath, have their children circumcised, celebrate the *Seder* on Passover Eve, and even observe *Yom Kippur*, the Day of Atonement. Keeping to the Jewish Law is optional (Stern, 1988). In the USA most men wear the *kippah* (skullcap) as a sign of their solidarity with the Jewish people, although it is enjoined in neither Scripture nor the Talmud (Schiffman, 1992). Baptism is practised, but the word 'baptism' is not used, because of its association for Jews with compulsory baptism; the word *mikveh* is preferred, the Jewish word for a ritual bath. They often have their own forms of worship, usually bowdlerised from Jewish liturgies. The movement is staffed not by Gentiles but by Jewish Christians. Their literature, such as I have seen of it, is focused on showing that Jesus is the Messiah, and the heir of the Old Testament. They have produced a book of testimonies from Jews who have become Messianic Jews (Rosen, 1987). They claim that for many Jews Judaism has ceased to be a living faith, but that it has now become a religion of their own cultural survival as a people.

As one would expect from an American source, the advertising is snappy and contemporary. 'Jews for Jesus – Established AD 32, Give Or Take A Year' is outside one headquarters, and 'Be More Jewish, Believe in Jesus' can be found in advertisements on the New York subway. (In 1992 the Jewish community, with the support of the *Church Times*, persuaded the London Underground authorities to remove similar advertisements from subway and trains.) Not unnaturally the Jewish authorities have launched organisations to counter this movement. As has been the case with other sects, there has been some excessive proselytising by Messianic Jews. There is some hard-sell American evangelism. It is said that Jewish Christianity is a sensible *via media* for mixed marriages between Christians and Jews – and nearly 50 per cent of Jews are said to 'marry out'. It is alleged that Russian Jews, recently arrived in New York, who know little about their faith after having been brought up under a communist regime and then emigrating to the USA, are told by Messianic Jews that real Jews believe in Jesus, and that they are offered English lessons and friendship. This is the kind of befriending which many parents have come to know to be the cause of the loss of their children to some fanatical sect. It is hardly surprising that Orthodox Jews have reacted to what they see as poaching. In New York there is a 'Jews for Judaism' group, and in one part of the city the Jewish Action Group of *Yad L'Achim* (aid to brothers) has organised weekly pickets at 'Jews for Jesus' services.

The movement has never caught on properly in Britain, for its style is distasteful, but 'Operation Judaism' has been formed in this country to oppose Jewish-oriented missionary work. There are some ten Jewish Christian congregations in Britain. They are not large, and they function like independent chapels. They keep Jewish festivals; and when I asked how Yom Kippur was observed in the light of Christ's atonement, I was told that the service contained mostly Bible readings of the Passion.

In Israel there are some forty Messianic Jewish congregations in the country, some in a Messianic Jewish *moshav*. Again, these congregations are independent, although recently a Messianic Action Committee has been set up to prevent enactment of a proposed law which would make it a criminal offence to possess any material which could be used to persuade others to change their religious affiliation. Such a law if passed would be strange in a State which calls itself secular, and in which people have freedom to practise or to change their religion. The development of these Messianic Jewish congregations in Israel is an important development. It is not due to any attempt by Gentile Christians to convert Jews to their faith. It is an indigenous movement among Jews who hope that other Jews will want to join them in their Jewish Christian faith without abandoning age-old Jewish traditions and customs. These congregations practise baptism, celebrate the Eucharist, and share in the Christian life which they celebrate as the fulfilment of their Judaism. The movement is still small, but evidently it has caused anxiety among the Orthodox who have promoted the bill mentioned above which is really aimed against Messianic Jews.

Messianic Jews in Israel should be distinguished from Biblical Zionists, who are Gentile Christians who believe that Jewish hegemony in Israel will hasten the Last Days. A visit to a Messianic Jewish *moshav* (like a kibbutz, but with children in family units) produced the following information. Each congregation is autonomous, and adopts the customs of various churches; Prebyterian, Baptist, etc. Most congregations have a religious leader. Some congregations construct their own liturgies. Baptism of adults is practised. Holy Communion is celebrated after baptisms, and at Jewish biblical feasts. Christian hymns have been translated, or Messianic Jewish hymns composed. Jewish music is not employed, as it is not centred on Jesus. The Christian Creeds are not used: the faith is centred on the New Testament. Jewish biblical festivals are kept, but interpreted messianically. Good Friday is observed on *Pesach*, the Jewish Passover. Circumcision is practised, and the Jewish Law is observed as laid down in the Scriptures (but not Talmudic law). Messianic Jews feel harassed and cut off from the Jewish community in Israel, as they are not regarded as real Jews; but they retain Jewish citizenship.

These Messianic Jewish congregations raise the important question: 'Who is a Jew?' Bernard Levin, himself a member of the Jewish race, has complained that he does not know. In Israel a Jew is a person who is so recognised by a Jewish authority. Under the Proclamation of Independence in 1948 'the State of Israel will be open to immigration and the ingathering of the exiles'. Under the Law of Return, entry is granted to any Jew who is recognised as such by any Jewish authority. There was a case of a Roman Catholic Jewish Christian priest who had spent his ministry in helping Jews and who wanted to settle in Israel. Although a way was found for him to do so, this was not allowed under the Law of the Return, because he was a Christian. Although Israel recognises as a Jew anyone who is recognised by any Jewish authority, unfortunately anyone who cannot prove to be the child of an Orthodox mother cannot be married in Israel, where only Orthodox Jewish weddings are permitted. 'Add to that the fact that the most liberal of the groupings within Judaism – the liberals and the progressives in Britain and the progressives in America – actually make it harder to be classed as a Jew if one had a Jewish mother but no Jewish upbringing, and one begins to tear out one's hair' (Neuberger, 1996). Under Islamic law it is not possible to change one's religion, which is regarded as given by birth. But Israel calls itself a secular State, and there is no legal obstacle to a Jewish citizen changing his or her religion, although a member of a non-Jewish religion, as we have seen, would not be given citizenship over the Law of Return.

In the Old Testament Jewish descent is calculated through the father, to judge from biblical genealogies. Ruth's Gentile blood was absorbed into the Jewish family into which she married – and King David, the archetypal Jew – was her grandson. However, in the course of time changed circumstances resulted in descent being calculated, in Orthodox Jewry, through the mother. A person is Jewish if the mother is Jewish. And so, in a mixed marriage, if the mother is a Jewess but her husband is a Gentile, the child is reckoned to be Jewish, but if it is the husband who is Jewish and his wife who is not, the child is not considered to be Jewish. In Liberal Judaism however descent may be calculated either through the father or through the mother. However if a Jew becomes a Christian, he or she is *beshummed*, a traitor, and no Orthodox family should have dealings with such a person: he or she is no longer regarded as a Jew.

It seems therefore that (as Jews see it) Jewishness is partly a matter of descent, and partly depends on a person not adhering to a religion other than Judaism. But that is not how Jewish Christians see it. They believe that it is simply a matter of descent, and that they can claim to be as Jewish as their fellow-Jews who profess the Jewish Faith; in fact they claim to be more Jewish, because their Jewish Faith is fulfilled in Jesus the Jew.

In this chapter I have attempted only to describe Messianic Judaism as it exists in the USA, Britain and Israel. (There are also Messianic Jewish congregations in Eastern Europe, and Richard Wurmbrand was a member of a Romanian congregation.) I have not given my own personal view of the movement: I reserve that for the succeeding chapter.

IO

A personal view

It has always seemed to me monstrous that Jews should be thought to be bound for hell because they do not believe in the Lord Jesus Christ. Really monstrous. I remember the occasion when I was due to be instituted as the Vicar of Great St Mary's, the University Church of Cambridge. In those days one was required by law to make a declaration to the effect that one believed the Thirty-Nine Articles of the Church of England were 'agreeable to the Word of God'. I could not do that. One of the articles states that 'works done before the grace of Christ, and the Inspiration of his Spirit, are not pleasing to God, for as much as they do not spring from faith in Jesus Christ' (Article 13). That would mean that everything done by my parents, and all my forebears and my cousins and brothers and aunts and all my Jewish friends were displeasing to God! I simply do not believe it. In the end, I hit upon the expedient of an additional declaration, in which I said that in assenting to the Articles as agreeable to the Word of God, I meant to the Word of God as it was understood at the time when they were composed. (Happily, the wording of the Declaration has now been changed.)

I think it is a *horrible* religion which supposes that all those who do not believe in Christ are bound for hell. I know goodness when I see it, and I have seen much goodness among Jews, among my relatives and others. St Paul declared that 'the fruit of the Spirit is love, joy, peace, longsuffering, gentleness, goodness, faith, meekness, and temperance: against such there is no law' (Gal. 5:22f.); and I have seen all these qualities in Jewish people. Christians who deny them salvation might call to mind the saying of Jesus: 'Not every one that saith unto me, Lord, Lord, shall enter into the kingdom of heaven, but he that doeth the will of my Father which is in heaven' (Matt. 7:21). I personally believe that since God is love, it is those who are permanently incapable of responding to love – if there be such – who are destined for damnation (or, if God is merciful, for decreation). It must be utterly terrible to live a loveless life as a person permanently incapable of responding to love: it does not require the punishment of hell, it is in itself the state of hell, and I hope and pray that if anyone is in that state they will simply cease to exist, i.e., be decreated by God.

How do I combine this with the belief that Jesus Christ died for our sins? Well, first, he died for the sins of the whole world; for *everyone*, not just for Christians who believe in him. His death and resurrection are God's way of taking action for us so that we can know that our sins have been forgiven, that we have all been accepted as his beloved sons and daughters, however bad we are. Yes, we have each to be able to accept for ourselves this truth in order that our reconciliation with God may become a reality; but that does not destroy its objectivity. Christ's death shows how seriously God takes our alienation from him, and the steps he has been prepared to take in Christ to ensure that we know how deeply he loves and accepts every one of us. Happily, I am very far from being the only person to believe that those who cannot accept Christ do not automatically go to hell. For example, this is no longer the belief of the Roman Catholic Church, which used to hold that all who did not belong to that particular Church were destined for damnation.

Pope John XXIII extensively revised the Roman Catholic prayer for Good Friday which is now 'For the Jews' instead of 'For the Conversion of the Jews'. In the Book of Common Prayer we used to pray on Good Friday for God to 'have mercy upon all Jews, Turks, Infidels and Hereticks, and upon all who have not known thee, or who deny the faith of Christ crucified. Take from them all ignorance, hardness of heart and contempt of thy Word, and so fetch them home . . .'. That prayer too has been revised, but only very modestly. According to the Alternative Service Book (1980), we now pray to God 'to have mercy upon your ancient people the Jews', and the prayer continues in more modern English in the same way as it did before. I am very uneasy about praying for Jews on Good Friday. It tends to perpetuate that terrible lie that it was the Jewish race that was responsible for the crucifixion of Jesus. All people need praying for, certainly; but not the Jews on Good Friday.

If the Jews are destined for salvation (and by that I mean that, if they can respond to love, they will eventually be in a situation where they are eternally with God and enjoy him for ever), what is the point of any attempt to bring to them the good news of Christ? Indeed, if salvation is possible without belief in Christ, was there any point in Christ's coming?

We could simply hold that all religions are equal, and that Jews worship God in one way, and Christians in another way, and one way is as good as the other. That has been said.

It is irrelevant how often one religion has tried to convert the members of another faith. What needs to be taken on board today is whether other religions have equality with one's own or not. If the answer is yes, then proselytising ceases as of right. If the answer is no, then the limit of tolerance has been reached, and we have to face the fact that the religion is not tolerant. It is in conversion activity, in statements that one form of salvation is best, to the exclusion of others, and in the quest for religious dominance of religion and in the provision of goods and services, that one has to draw the line. (Neuberger, 1996)

This seemed to me to be a muddled statement, and I think that it was this that finally decided me to write this book. First, proselytism means putting undue pressure on people to convert: it is to be sharply distinguished from reasoned argument, against which I can see in principle no possible objection. Second, those who live in glass houses shouldn't throw stones. Rabbi Neuberger is attacking the Church of England over what she calls 'religious dominance of education'. I deal with this later in the chapter, but here let me simply point out that Judaism has far more 'religious dominance of education' in Israel than the Church of England has in Britain, a country whose government actually gives financial support to schools specifically for young Jewish boys and girls. Third, as I have pointed out earlier, I cannot understand the claim that all religions are equal, and that no way of salvation is better than another. Should we include the form of religion known as Satanism here? And some of the more obnoxious forms of sects, like the one which tried to poison Japanese in their underground railways? Is there to be no religious discrimination whatsoever? Are there no questions of truth involved? It seems to me that either Jesus was a mere man, or he was not. Either Mohammed superseded Judaism and Christianity, or he did not. If all is relative, truth goes out of the door. I cannot help feeling that the writer has been unduly influenced by the Enlightenment to write such stuff. I have to bear witness for myself to the conviction that, for all the blessings which I received as a boy and adolescent through Jewish worship, the Christian approach to God through Christ is better. I do not believe that this is an instance of intolerance. Of course I respect other people's religious views, but to disagree with them is not intolerant.

It would be foolish for me to pretend that I do not want Jews to know Jesus Christ as their Lord and Saviour. Of course I do. How could I do otherwise, seeing the blessings that I have received through him? I am well aware that believing Jews have a real personal relationship with God, that he is a reality in their lives, and that their lives can be transformed by him: this book is in part a testimony to this truth. Moreover, Jews certainly believe in the same God as Christians. I myself have found that I can know God better through Christ, because Christ was a human being transparent to God, and if I look to him, I can see God translated, as it were, into terms of human personality. I have always felt, from the very first moments of my conversion, that far from there being any essential opposition between Judaism and Christianity, the latter for me was the fulfilment of the former. But if Jews wish to remain as Jews without Christ – and, God knows! there are good reasons for them to do this – then they must be respected as persons made in God's image, and I must leave the matter to God. They are quite right to stay in the religion in which God has placed them until such time as they may find it incomplete.

I am not, by writing this, denying the importance of Christian mission. Christianity is a religion of which mission has a vital part. Here I must repeat what I have written elsewhere, because I cannot put it better:

> Mission is an integral part of the Gospel. The word means in origin a 'being sent', and was originally used of the Trinity: the Father 'sent' the Son into the world, and the Spirit too was 'sent' into the world. Sending is therefore integral to the Gospel. Christians are members of the Church sent into the world to do God's will. To deny mission is therefore to deny the good news which they bring. What mission consists of and how it is actually accomplished are more complex matters. Mission includes all forms of Christian service in the world; among these the healings ministry, the personal acts of service which Christians render to non-Christians, as well as social action at a corporate level undertaken by Christians as a way of serving their fellow men and women (for example, by provision of schools for children or hospices for the dying, and the provision of wells and clean water in developing countries). Even this does not exhaust Christian mission. Christians are sent into the world to be as well as to act. The very presence of Christian men and women, leading the Christian life and showing love and kindness to their fellow men and women, forms an important part of mission.
>
> One vital aspect of mission is evangelism, which is the sharing of the Good News of Christ with others, and especially with those who have no faith in God. There are many ways of evangelism (in the sense of sharing the Christian faith). This must be distinguished from proselytism, which involves manipulating people into the Christian faith and which is an offence against their integrity. In some situations the liturgy is a powerful form of evangelism. There are situations (e.g. towards the Jewish

people) where evangelism is better accomplished not by naming the name of Christ but simply through manifesting the love of God through personal life style. (Montefiore, 1993)

Why do I say that it is better not to name the name of Christ to my fellow-Jews? Not all my fellow-Christians would agree with this, and not all my Jewish fellow-Christians. But I believe it is better not to name the name of Christ to Jews because down the centuries the word Christ has been a curse to them, causing discrimination against them, forfeiture of possessions, social deprivation, civic disabilities and even torture and death. So the name of Christ has become the very reverse of good news: it is bad news. Even if present circumstances are favourable, the events of the past are still indelibly imprinted in the Jewish folk memory. When a generation arises, if it does, in which these past events are no longer in the folk memory, the situation will be different.

I fear that Christians have not been outstanding in extending the hand of genuine friendship to members of the Jewish people. There are some splendid exceptions, but the exceptions, alas, only prove the rule. I think that 'manifesting the love of God through personal life style', as I have called it, is best done by individuals rather than by whole congregations. If the latter, it will seem to Jewish people that this is a kind of gimmick to make them become Christians, whereas what is intended is a genuine loving attitude which has no ulterior motive other than to love others because God loves us. And, when one considers the past, there is an awful lot of loving that is needed if it is in any way to atone for the terrible hating which has taken place in the past.

At the same time I do sometimes think that the Jewish community is being somewhat oversensitive over any moves by Christians to enable Jews to accept Jesus as the Christ. Undue pressure brought upon any set of people to get them to accept a religion is immoral, and I can well understand and indeed sympathise with those who object to that. But for a Christian to tell a Jew about what he or she understands to be the good news of Christ if the Jew wants to hear this – what is wrong in principle with that? We live in a free country, and we are surely free to say what we like to one another, so long as it is not racialist and so long as it is acceptable to the other person to hear it. One would have thought that Jews might welcome the opportunity to stick up for their own tenets when confronted by Christian beliefs. No doubt centuries of harassment makes them feel that this would not even yet be an equal contest. I think that perhaps this oversensitivity on the subject of Christian evangelism is a symptom of their continuing insecurity.

So what do I think of modern movements of Messianic Jews in the USA and in Israel? I know that they are not for me. I am disinclined to pass judgment on people who live in a situation very different from myself. I find aspects of the American movement manipulative. It seems so often 'hard sell' propaganda and I recoil from what seems to me cheap, even if effective, propaganda. Maybe this does not seem the case to Americans. But it does to me.

I am sure I could not join a Messianic Jewish group in Britain. I realise that a handful do exist. My reasons are manifold. Firstly I am primarily a Christian who happens to be Jewish, rather than a Jew who believes that Jesus was the Messiah. Then Messianic Jewish congregations seem to operate like independent chapels, while I value the historic ministry of the Church. I prefer to belong to a local embodiment of the One Holy Catholic Church, linked with the greater worldwide church. Secondly I do not want to worship simply with Jews. For me, Jesus has broken down the middle wall of partition between Jews and Gentiles. I gather that there are some Gentile Christians in these Messianic Jewish assemblies. But what are they doing there? Why should they wish to keep Jewish festivals and fasts, and share in a Jewish Christian liturgy? I can only imagine that they are disaffected from some institutional church to which they formerly belonged.

I appreciate however that my personal convictions on this matter are not shared by all Jewish Christians. After reading the testimonies of other Jews who have become Christians (Fieldsend, 1993), I can understand better why they feel differently from myself. They have so often been brought up to fear and shun the name of Jesus:

somehow it sounds different to them if he is called his Hebrew name Y'shua. Christ has almost become his surname in Church circles; and so they prefer to call him the Hebrew Messiah. The Gentile atmosphere of the Christian Church is so alien to them that they feel more at home in a Messianic Jewish setting. They are able to continue to use some of their beloved Jewish prayers, and say the Shema' together. They feel that in worshipping in this way that they are continuing to be Jews as well as embracing Christianity. They have a strong feeling of solidarity not only with one another, but also with the whole Jewish race.

Some Messianic Jews feel that they are members of the righteous 'remnant' which features in the Old Testament (Schiffman, 1992). The doctrine of the remnant is that through the faithfulness of the few salvation will come to all. It was so with Elijah: 'the people of Israel have forsaken thy covenant, torn down thy altars and put thy prophets to death by the sword. I alone am left' (1 Kings 19:14 NEB). The prophet Isaiah actually called his son Shear-jashub, which means 'a remnant shall return'. As he explained: 'A remnant shall return again, a remnant of Jacob, to God their champion. Your people, Israel, shall be many as the sands of the sea, but only a remnant shall turn again' (Isa. 10:21f. NEB). Is it possible that Jewish Christians are the remnant of Israel through whom God will save the whole Jewish people? I know that I have been called to follow Christ, but as a Jewish Christian I do not feel that I belong to the 'righteous remnant' of Israel, as in the Old Testament, through whom the whole future Jewish people will be saved from destruction. This would imply that the Jews are to be blamed for not having turned to Christ as their Saviour, whereas the facts are that Christians have behaved so intolerably towards them that for many the name of Christ is anathema.

Messianic Jews may not be the 'righteous remnant', but it is certainly true that if Jewish Christianity is to flourish, this is only likely to come about through the Christian character and way of life of Jews who have become Christians. When compared with the total number of Jews in the world, the number of 'Messianic Jews' is not very impressive. But they are increasing quite rapidly;

faster now, I have been informed, than any other non-Jewish ethnic group. While I myself continue to believe that the best way of ministering to Jews is not to name the name of Jesus, I can understand that those who adopt a more evangelical stance wish to share their faith with other Jews, and to help them by introducing them to their Jewish Christian worship.

As for the Messianic Jewish movement in Israel, that is rather another matter. I am personally not attracted to the closed kind of society that necessarily must exist on a kibbutz, but it is not necessary for such assemblies to be confined to such communities. I can understand that Jewish Christians in Israel do not want to cut themselves off from the Jewish communities to which they belong (although of course by acknowledging Jesus as Messiah they have done just that). Nor do they want to cut themselves off from their Jewish inheritance. But the same objections would hold for me in Israel as in this country. I personally do not want to belong to self-governing conventicles which function rather like independent chapels. I am very happy to worship with Christian fundamentalists, but I do not want to belong to a Christian group in which fundamentalism is written into its title deeds. And I want to worship with my fellow-Christians who are not Jews as well as with those who are Jews. What about the Arab Christians and expatriate Christians in Israel? Surely those who are Christians should show solidarity when the racial groups to which they belong are opposed to one another? And I would find it difficult to keep Saturday as a special day and not Sunday along with my fellow-Christians. It would be difficult to keep both the Feast of Tabernacles and a Christian harvest festival, but I think it would be possible to combine the two. I would find it hard to keep Yom Kippur because I believe that it has been superseded by Good Friday. But if I lived in Israel, yes, I think I would feel an urge to join a Jewish Christian assembly, but my head would rule my heart. It is a hypothetical situation for me. I do not live in Israel, and as I shall explain, I no longer wish even to visit the country.

Naturally I wish that all Jews would become Christians, in Israel and elsewhere; but I realise that this is a dream and not a practicality.

For better or for worse, both Christianity and Judaism have gone their own separate ways since those early days when the first Christian disciples maintained their own strong table fellowship in Christ, and at the same time worshipped regularly in the Jewish Temple. Christianity has (to my mind) fossilised its creeds within Hellenistic metaphysical categories, and Gentile assumptions have overwhelmed important Jewish insights. It has engaged in over-definition of dogma and heresy, and has tended to put its traditions on the same level as scriptural revelation. Judaism too has not stood still. It has developed its own way of life, with overdefinition not of dogma but of orthopraxy, and again tradition has tended to be put on a par with scriptural revelation. Add to this the prejudices against Jesus Christ incurred by the abominable way in which Christians have treated Jews, and it seems almost beyond the realm of possibility that the two Faiths could ever merge; and even if they did, this would probably produce a third faith, because in such a case there would be bound to be 'continuing Christians' and 'continuing Jews'. But of course miracles can happen, and no prediction is certain.

Things being as they are, I am a realist and I very much want Judaism to continue. We must all follow our consciences. Jews are called to be good Jews, observant of the Faith in which God has placed them. Judaism should be honoured and respected by all Christians. Judaism has much to show the world. It is a living example of death and resurrection. It is a witness to the election and providence of God. It is a reminder of the historical origins of our Faith. It provides a way of life that must surely be pleasing to God. Its worship shows a spirit of gratitude and thankfulness to God so often absent in other Faiths. It has a very high ethic (although Jews do not observe it any more than Christians observe theirs). Christians should welcome the presence of a Jewish community in their midst, and encourage good relations between its members and theirs. When I read how Arabs extinguished thriving and talented Jewish and Christian communities as *dhimmi* under Arab rule in the Orient (Ye'or, 1996), it seems to me to be incumbent on intolerant Christians to be much more positive in their approach to those of other Faiths in our so-called Christian society.

I feel a Jew as well as a Christian. Does that mean that I feel I have to keep the Jewish food laws? No, it does not. Even Liberal Jews do not keep them nowadays. I take seriously Article 7 of the Thirty-Nine Articles: 'Although the Law given from God by Moses, as touching Ceremonies and Rites, do not bind Christian men, nor the Civil precepts thereof ought of necessity to be received in any commonwealth; yet notwithstanding, no Christian man whatsoever is free from the obedience of the Commandments which are called Moral.' Not that the Law was given directly by God to Moses, nor are all the commandments which are called moral valid today. For example, had either of my brothers died without children, I would have felt no obligation to marry their widows in order 'to raise up seed' for my brothers! As a Christian I feel set free from the Jewish ritual Law, and from the literal interpretation of the Jewish moral Law. For example, I do not feel under an obligation to keep the Sabbath from sunset on Friday to sunset on Saturday: I am happy to keep it on a Sunday. At the same time there are moral precepts of the utmost importance to be found in the Old Testament which are fundamental for the regulation of human behaviour.

What of Jewish festivals? I enjoy participating when I am asked to a Jewish Seder service on Passover Eve, and even attending once in a while Jewish Morning or Evening Service, because some of the prayers are so lovely and moving, and I find a note of thanksgiving and gratitude in them which I do not find very often in Christian worship. I have no difficulty whatsoever in joining in the Jewish prayers. But I do not feel called to observe them as a matter of spiritual discipline.

Should I have married a Jewish Christian instead of a Gentile? Interestingly enough I don't think I knew a single such girl at the time of my marriage, although I have met several since then. In any case in Christ Jew and Gentile are one, and I do not think that there can be any theological reason why Jewish Christians should marry one another instead of a Gentile Christian. But the inevitable result of such a 'mixed marriage' is that the children are very unlikely to know about their Jewish inheritance, especially if their mother is not Jewish. Their children – the grandchildren of the Jewish Christian spouse – will be even less likely to know about this. And so the Jewishness will be lost within the overwhelmingly Gentile character of the Christian Church. This is inevitable, if sad. It is perhaps more than sad, because Jewish spirituality, as I have indicated earlier in this book, has at times something to teach Christian spirituality, which would be the richer for absorbing it. For this reason the Christian Church could pay special attention to Jewish Christians if they make suggestions out of their Jewishness about the liturgy, or about over-definition of doctrine, or even about excessive Christocentrism.

What of the State of Israel? I find this, as do many people, a very difficult problem. Whenever I have visited the Holy Land I have not felt that I wanted to settle there but I have experienced not only a feeling of joy that I am walking where Jesus trod, but also a sense of pleasure that I am back in my own homeland, where my own roots lie, in land promised centuries and centuries ago to my very, very distant forebears. It is noticeable how Americans love to visit the places in Ireland or England from which their ancestors set out to a new life in America. In a sense they feel that they have come home. But their ancestors left their homeland voluntarily, even if it was because they could not find a livelihood there. However, the Jews left involuntarily, and the joy of return must therefore be all the greater.

I can understand that a certain ruthlessness was necessary to start a country as it were from scratch. I can appreciate the longing of Jews for a national home, somewhere where they can actually feel safe and secure, an asylum and a homeland. After all that Jews have suffered down the centuries, surely it is appropriate that they should once more live in the land which they believe that God has given them in an everlasting covenant? At the same time, God has not laid down exactly what the frontiers of that land should be, and it cannot be justly claimed that all the occupied territory seized in 1967 in the Six Days War is part of the Jewish inalienable inheritance.

A personal view

In defence of Israel it must be admitted that the Arab occupants of the land were encouraged by other countries to flee when Israel's independence was declared. It is true too that some land had been legally purchased earlier from Arabs. Large numbers of Jews have emigrated to Israel from Arab countries, but at the same time huge numbers of Arabs have to live in refugee camps, dispossessed of their land. Furthermore, there probably is some real justification for the Jewish fear of their Arab neighbours. It must be very provoking for Arabs in neighbouring states to have in their midst a country no longer predominantly Muslim but Jewish, and also an ally of the USA, now the only world superpower. Not all the surrounding Arab countries have yet made peace with Israel twenty years after hostilities have ceased. Israelis will know that the earlier history of Islam suggests that when Muslims have had power (and until their oil runs out Arab countries will continue to have power) they have dealt with those of other faiths either by *jihad* (holy war) or by *dhimma* (subservient status). And did not the surrounding Muslim countries threaten to drive the Israelis in the sea? The PLO have now stated that death will be the punishment for any Arab selling land to a Jew.

But at the same time the Jews, no doubt haunted by insecurity, have reacted to their neighbours in what seems to an outsider to be a somewhat foolish manner, encouraging them to harden their opposition rather than taking steps to mitigate it. If there is to be peace in the Middle East there must be confidence and trust, and these are the fruit not of intransigence but of sympathy and understanding. The Israelis, by behaving in a way which appears to others as arrogant and aggressive, seem to encourage the Arabs to hate them, instead of stretching out the hand of fellowship to them as their brothers and sisters, the descendants of Jacob befriending the children of Esau. (Interestingly enough, it is the more recent immigrants rather than the *sabras* (Israeli-born Jews) who are usually the most aggressive.) I feel that the only permanent solution will be a form of binationalism or joint rule in Israel and the occupied territories, but that seems at the moment a very distant if not impossible goal.

When I am with Jews in the Holy Land, I feel deep sympathy with them, and rejoice that they are living again in their own land; but when I am with Arabs I feel appalled at the second class status which seems so often to be accorded to them. Such is my feeling of distress, that unlike Moses Montefiore who wanted to make his eighth pilgrimage there in his ninety-third year, I do not feel that I wish to return there ever again.

And what of Jews who live in the Diaspora? Their roots are now no longer in the Holy Land but in the countries in which they were born. They are not strangers and aliens in these countries of the *Galuth*: they are full citizens, with the full rights of citizens. Most of them naturally want to play their full part in these countries; and they want to stay there. This is now their personal decision. They could, if they so wished, emigrate to Israel under the Law of Return. If they stay in the country in which they were born, and if that country has a Christian tradition (even if in some ways it may seem to be in a post-Christian phase), they must accept these traditions based upon a Christian past. The Church of England is still the established church of the land, and the Chief Rabbi of the United Synagogues, in his Reith Lectures, approved of this situation (Sacks, 1991). Since it is the tradition of this country that each day school should start with an act of worship in an assembly, and that there should be lessons of religious education, I do not think that it should be a cause for complaint that the religion concerned should be predominantly Christian, although complaints have been made (Neuberger, 1996). Because this country upholds liberal values in education, it is possible for parents who object to this to withdraw their children from assembly and from lessons of religious education. This is what happened to me before I became a Christian, and I did not feel any embarrassment in so doing.

Those who comprise a minority religion in a country may react in one of two ways. They can maintain a tight community, with few contacts outside it, and send their children to schools which hold their minority faith. Or they can mix in an open way with the larger community, and take their full share in social and other activities. The Jewish community, which used to take the former course, has now largely opted for the latter. The consequences of so doing must be faced. Large numbers marry non-Jews, there is assimilation to Christian customs (keeping Christmas is a case in point), and there is a loss of dynamic in the keeping of an ancestral faith. This is what is now happening to a large percentage of the Jewish people in Britain, a fact to which the Chief Rabbi has not infrequently drawn attention. It is sad, because a strong Jewish community is an asset to this country, and that strength will wither if the present drift continues. The ending of intolerance, paradoxically, has not helped the Jewish community.

I would not wish to end this book however on such a negative note. In the West, we are living in an increasingly godless world. It is becoming very commonly held that the natural sciences have overturned theistic belief, although in fact the opposite is the truth. Secularisation means the privatisation of religious belief, which becomes a mere option like the choice of a brand in a supermarket. What is true tends to give way to what I want or what I like. Consumerism is engulfing our natural resources and polluting our planet in such a way as to endanger the future of living things, including human life. We are losing that sense of common values which is based on Judaeo-Christian theistic belief, so that our communities tend to disintegrate, the family tends to be disrupted by divorce, and to judge by the media the country seems obsessed with sex.

Judaism and Christianity have common beliefs which could be powerful in reversing this trend. Our common commitment to the living God as the creator of the universe and its redeemer and sanctifier, our common conviction that human beings are made in the image of God and therefore always to be respected and honoured, our common belief that God created the world, and that we humans have a duty to care for it, not to wreck it: these are vital for the future well-being of our society. On these matters Judaism and Christianity can go hand in hand. Jews and Christians have far more important things to do together than merely to stop anti-Semitism (although that is important). They can co-operate in stemming the disintegration of our culture and filling the spiritual void in our society. Although Jews and Christians are on some matters far apart, on others they are close together, and in these they can work together for the welfare of all. As Archbishop Lord Coggan said in St Paul's Cathedral on the fiftieth anniversary of the Council of Christians and Jews in 1992:

> It will at once be said that there are differences between the Jewish and the Christian faith. Indeed there are, and they are big and many; those differences must continue to be the heart of ongoing dialogue. But mother (Judaism) and daughter (Christianity) have so much in common which is essential to the very life of the world that we should regard it as the truth of which we are common trustees together and together we should make its light shine. We have a common message and, I would dare to say, a common mission.

The two faiths not only have a common message and mission: they need one another. Martin Buber wrote:

> Jewish *Emunah* is the state of persevering – also to be called trust in the existential sense – of man in an invisible guidance which yet gives itself to be seen in a hidden but self-revealing guidance. Christian *Pistis* was born outside the historical experience of nations, so to say on retirement from history, in the souls of individuals to whom the challenge came to believe that a man crucified in Jerusalem was their saviour . . . An Israel striving after the renewal of its faith through the rebirth of the person, and a Christianity striving for the renewal of nations through the rebirth of the person would have something as yet unsaid to give to one another – hardly to be conceived at the present time. (Buber, 1951)

James Parkes presented a similar idea in less philosophical language when he wrote: 'That highest purpose of God which Sinai reveals to man in community, Calvary reveals to man as an end in itself' (Parkes, 1948). And a little later he added: 'The Christian religion is a mystery of salvation, and it converts by winning man simply to its life and teaching. Judaism is a way of life to the nations among which and within which it lives.' He ends the chapter with these words:

> We need both Judaism and Christian, for the sufferings of the present time are such that no explanation of them both could be too profound, or could link too closely the whole fabric of the universe. In Judaism God says to man: fulfil my plan for creation; and man replies; I will. In Christianity man returns to God to say: fulfil that part in creation which I cannot because I am foolish and sinful; and God replies: I will. In Judaism and Christianity together the 'I–Thou' relationship of a free creation is ultimately fulfilled. But in each is an essential part of the fulfilment, and until there appears a way by which they can fulfil the two together without losing their essential nature, each must fulfil its own part. But the better the Jew or the Christian can understand the religion of the other the better its own task can be fulfilled.

Yes, indeed. But until the day comes when Judaism and Christianity can go arm in arm, cannot Jewish Christians help in contributing to the Church what only the Synagogue can give?

Glossary of Jewish words

'Adon 'olam	'Lord over all', hymn at Morning Prayer
Ain kelorhainu	'There is none like our God', hymn at Morning Prayer
'aleph	first letter of the Hebrew alphabet
'am ha-aretz	the people of the land
Amidah	an ancient prayer of thanksgiving and supplication
Amoraim	teachers of the Law, coming after the Tannaim, responsible for the Talmud
afikomen	piece of matsah set aside during the Passover seder
Ashkenazim	Jews from Eastern Europe
barmitzvah	a boy's passage to adulthood at thirteen
beshummed	traitor – Jew who becomes a Christian
dayenu	'it would be sufficient for us' – prayer or song for Passover eve
echal	the Ark holding the *Sepher Torah*
eruv	an enclosed area exempt from the rules of a sabbath day's journey
galuth	dispersion, the Diaspora
Gush Emunim	a society which believes that the land of Israel is the gift of God to the Jews
haftorah	a reading from the prophets

Halachah	teaching of the rabbis
Hallel	joyful psalms sung at Passover
Hanuccah,	feast commemorating the Maccabees
haroset	sweet food made from almonds, apples and other fruits used at Passover
Hasid (pl. Hasidim)	a member of a Jewish sect founded in the 18th century, emphasising joy in the presence of God
herem	'the ban', total destruction of the booty of war, as an offering to God in ancient Israel
hoopah	canopy under which stand bride and groom at a wedding
Kabbala	'tradition', the secret mystical tradition of the Middle Ages
Kaddish	prayer for the dead
kal vahomer	'If this, how much more that', an *a fortiori* argument used in rabbinic ethics
Karaites	a Jewish sect which recognises the regulations of the Bible, but not of the Talmud
kibbutz	Israeli settlement (now non-existent) in which all the children were brought up in a communal unit
Kiddush	blessing said before a meal on sabbaths and festivals
Kiddush Hashem	sanctification of God's name in Jewish ethics
kippah	skullcap
kosher	food prepared according to scriptural and Talmudic laws
lulab	branches waved at the feast of Tabernacles
Mahammad	synagogue council
maneh	ancient Israelite money equivalent to a hundred *shekels*
Manishtanah	question asked by the youngest at Passover
Manserim	children of incest or adultery

matzah, pl. *matzoth*	unleavened bread
mezuzoth	small metal cylinders containing texts from Deuteronomy
mikveh	ritual bath at the end of menstruation
minyan	quorum of ten males needed for worship on the Sabbath
Mishnah	collection of the contents of the oral law, basis of the Talmud
mitzvot	duties, e.g., those assumed at barmitzvah
mokh	a contraceptive barrier
moshav	community in which the children are cared for in family units
parasha	portion of the Pentateuch used in worship
Pesach	Passover
Purim	'Lots', a feast commemorating Esther's rescue of the Jews of Persia
Rosh Hashana	Jewish New Year's Day
Sabra	an Israeli-born Jew
Sanhedrin	council
Seder	the order of service for Passover night
Sephardim	Jews from Spain, North Africa and Yemen
Sepher Torah	scroll of the Law
shamayim	heaven
Shekinah	the radiant glory of God, his presence
Shema'	the Jewish prayer from Deut. 4:6-9
shevarim	succession of three notes on the *shofar*
Shoah	the Holocaust
shofar	the ram's horn blown on *Rosh Hashana*
Sifre	Commentaries on Numbers and Deuteronomy by Tannaitic rabbis
succah	a booth
Succoth	the feast of Booths, or Tabernacles
taleth	prayer shawl used by men in the synagogue
Talmud	commentary on the Mishnah
Tannaim	literally Teachers, applied to rabbis from AD 10 to 220

tebah	reading desk for the *sepher Torah*
teshubhah	conversion
Torah	books of the Law
Targum	Aramaic paraphrase of the Hebrew scriptures once read in the synagogue
tekiah	sustained blast on the *shofar*
teruah	succession of short trills on the *shofar*
Y'shua	Jesus
yetzer hara'	the evil impulse
yetzer hatob	the good impulse
Yom kippur	Day of Atonement
zedakah	righteousness, justice, almsgiving

Bibliography

Books quoted or alluded to in the text.

Barker, M. *The Great Angel* (SPCK, 1992).

Baum, G., *The Jews and the Gospel* (Bloomsbury Press, 1960).

Bayfield, T. and M. Braybrooke (eds), *Dialogue with Difference* (SCM Press, 1992).

Berkovits, E., *Faith after the Holocaust* (Ktav, New York, 1973).

Braybrooke, M., *Time to Meet* (SCM Press, 1990).

Buber, M., *Two Types of Faith* (Routledge & Kegan Paul, 1951).

Buber, M., *Israel and Palestine* (East and West Library, 1952).

Buber, M., *Werke 1* (Munich/Heidelberg, 1962), quoted by The Declaration of German Catholic Bishops on the Church's Relationship to Judaism, 1980.

Cohen, A., *Everyman's Talmud* (Dent, 1932).

Cohen, L., *Some Recollections of Claude Goldsmid Montefiore* (Faber, 1950).

Cohn-Sherbok, D., *The Crucified Jew* (HarperCollins, 1992).

Cooper, H., and P. Morrison, *A Sense of Belonging* (Weidenfield & Nicholson, 1991).

Dix, G., *Jew and Greek* (Dacre, 1953).

Dodd, C. H., *According to the Scriptures* (Nisbet, 1952).

Driver, S. R., and A. Neubauer, *The 53rd Chapter of Isaiah and Its Jewish Interpreters* (Parker, 1876).

Eckardt, A. L., 'Post Holocaust Theology: A Journey out of the

Kingdom of Night', *Holocaust and Genocide Studies*, Vol. 1, No. 2 (Pergamon Press, 1986).

Eckardt, A. R., 'Salient Jewish Christian Issues Today: A Christian Exploration' in J. H. Charlesworth (ed.), *Jews and Christians*, (Crossroad, 1990).

Ecclestone, A., *The Night Sky of the Lord* (Darton, Longman and Todd, 1980).

Ellison, H. L., 'The Church and the Hebrew Christian' in G. Hedenquist (ed.), *The Church and the Jewish People* (Edinburgh House Press, 1954).

Elmslie, W. A. L., 'Ethics' in H. Wheeler Robinson (ed.), *Record and Revelation* (Oxford University Press, 1938).

Epstein, I., *Judaism* (Penguin Books, 1959).

Feldman, H., 'Palestinian and Diaspora Judaism in the First Century' in H. Shanks (ed.), *Christianity and Rabbinic Judaism* (SPCK, 1993).

Fieldsend, J., *Messianic Jews* (Monarch Publications, 1993).

Fiorenza, E. F. and D. Tracey (eds), *The Holocaust as Interruption* (*Concilium*, T & T Clark, 1984).

Friedlander, A., *Leo Baeck* (Routledge & Kegan Paul, 1973).

Friedlander, A., *Against the Fall of Night* (Council of Christians and Jews, 1984).

Friedlander, A., 'The Geography of Theology' in T. Bayfield and M. Braybrooke (eds.) *Dialogue with a Difference* (SCM Press, 1992).

Fry, H. P. (ed.), *Christian–Jewish Dialogue: A Reader* (Exeter University Press, 1996).

Gilbert, M., *The Holocaust* (Collins, 1986).

Gillet, L., *Judaism and Christianity* (Shears, 1939).

Gillet, L., *Communion in the Messiah* (Lutterworth, 1942).

Goldhagen, D. J., *Hitler's Willing Executioners: Ordinary Germans and the Holocaust* (Vintage Books, New York, 1997).

Grollenberg, L., *Palestine Comes First* (SCM Press, 1979).

Grollenberg, L., *Unexpected Messiah* (SCM Press, 1988).

Guinness, M., *A Little Kosher Seasoning* (Hodder & Stoughton, 1994).

Gutteridge, J., *Open My Mouth to the Dumb* (Blackwell, 1976).

Bibliography

Harwood, R. G. *Did Six Million Really Die?* (Historical Review Press, nd).

Hick, J., *An Interpretation of Religion* (Macmillan, 1989).

Houlden, J. L., *Jesus, A Question of Identity* (SCM Press, 1992).

Hyamson, A. M., *A History of the Jewish People in England* (Methuen, 1928).

Jocz, J., *The Jewish People and Jesus Christ* (SPCK, 1949).

Johnson, A., *The One and the Many in the Israelite Conception of God* (University of Wales Press Board, 1942).

Johnson, P., *A History of the Jews* (Weidenfeld & Nicholson, 1987).

Kessler, E., (ed.), *An English Jew: The Life and Writings of Claude Montefiore* (Vallentine Mitchell, 1989).

Koestler, A., *The Thirteenth Tribe* (Hutchinson, 1976).

Küng, H., *Judaism* (SCM Press, 1992).

Lelyweld, A., *Atheism is Dead* (World Publishing Co., 1968).

Levertoff, O., 'Paul Levertoff and the Jewish Christian Problem' in L. Gillet (ed.), *Judaism and Christianity* (Shears, 1939).

Levison, L., 'Address on election as first President of the Hebrew Christian Alliance' in H. Schonfield, *The History of Jewish Christianity* (Duckworth, 1936).

Loewe, H., *Diaries of Sir Moses and Lady Montefiore* (Jewish Historical Society of England, 1983).

Maccoby, H., 'Myth and Morality' in T. Bayfield and M. Braybrooke (ed.), *Dialogue with a Difference* (SCM Press, 1992).

Manson, T. W., *Jesus and the Non-Jews* (Athlone Press, 1955).

Marcus, J., *Jesus and the Holocaust* (Doubleday, 1997).

Martini, C. M., in *Jews and Christians* (Crossroad, 1990).

Montefiore, C. G., *Outlines of Liberal Judaism* (Macmillan, 1923).

Montefiore, C. G., *The Synoptic Gospels* (Macmillan, 1927).

Montefiore, H., *Credible Christianity* (Cassell, 1993).

Neuberger, J., *On Being Jewish* (Mandarin Press, 1996).

Oesterley, W. O. E., 'The Jewish Liturgy' in L. Gillet, *Judaism and Christianity* (Shears, 1939).

Parkes, J., *Conflict of the Church and the Synagogue* (Soncino Press, 1934).

Parkes, J., *Judaism and Christianity* (Gollancz, 1948).

Rengstorf, K. H., 'The Jewish Problem and the Church's Understanding of its own Mission' in G. Hedenquist (ed.), *The Church and the Jewish People* (Edinburgh House Press, 1954).

Reuther, R., *Faith and Fratricide* (Seabury, New York, 1979).

Rosen, R., (ed.), *Jesus for Jews* (Messianic Jewish Perspective Publications, San Francisco, 1987).

Roth, C., *History of the Jewish People 1600-1935* (Macmillan, 1936).

Rubinstein, R., 'The Condition of Human Belief' in *Commentary* (New York, 1966).

Rubinstein, W.D., *The Myth of Rescue: Why the Democracies Could not Have saved More Jews From the Nazis* (Routledge, 1997).

Sacks, J., *The Persistence of Faith* (Weidenfeld & Nicholson, 1991).

Sanders, E. P., *Jesus and Judaism* (SCM Press, 1985).

Sanders, J., *Schismatics, Sectarians, Dissidents, Deviants* (SCM Press, 1993).

Schiffman, M., *Return of the Remnant* (Lederer Publications, 1992).

Schoeps, H. J., *The Jewish Christian Argument* (Faber, 1965).

Schonfield, H., *The History of Jewish Christianity* (Duckworth, 1936).

Shriver, D. W., *An Ethic for Enemies* (Oxford University Press, New York, 1995).

Smith, R., 'The Christian Message' in G. Hedenquist (ed.), *The Church and the Jewish People* (Edinburgh House Press, 1954).

Snape, R. H., 'Rabbinical and Early Christian Ethics', in C. G. Montefiore and H. Loewe, *A Rabbinic Anthology* (Macmillan, 1938).

Stern, D. H., *Messianic Jewish Manifesto* (Jewish New Testament Publications, Israel, 1988).

Svidercoschi, G. F., *Letter to a Jewish Friend* (Hodder and Stoughton, 1994).

Taylor, V., *Jesus and His Sacrifice* (Macmillan, 1951).

Tutunji, J., Khaldi, K., 'Binationalism: the rational and moral choice', in *International Affairs* (Cambridge University Press, Jan. 1997).

Underhill, E., *Mysticism* (Methuen, 1923).

Vermes, G., *Jesus and the World of Judaism* (SCM Press, 1983).

Wade, G. W., *The Book of the Prophet Isaiah* (Methuen, 1929).

Wiebe, P. H., *Visions of Jesus* (Oxford University Press, New York, 1997).

Bibliography

Wiesel, E., *Night* (Penguin, 1981).

Wilken, R. L., *John Chrysostom and the Jews* (University of California, 1983).

World Council of Churches, *The Theology of the Churches and the Jewish People: Statements by the World Council of Churches and its Member Churches* (WCC Publications, 1988).

Wyman, D. S., *The Abandonment of the Jews* (Random House, 1984).

Ye'or, B., *The Decline of Eastern Christianity under Islam* (Associated University Presses, 1996).

Zimmels, H. T., *Ashkenazim and Sephardim* (Oxford University Press, 1958).

The Truth Shall Make You Free: The Lambeth Conference Report (Church House Publishing, 1988).

Report on Jewish/Christian Dialogue of the Overseas Council of the Church of Scotland, (Church of Scotland, 1980).

Permissions

Extracts from the *Book of Common Prayer*, the rights in which are vested in the Crown, are reproduced by permission of the Crown's Patentee, Cambridge University Press.

Extracts from the *Authorized Version of the Bible (The King James Bible)*, the rights in which are vested in the Crown, are reproduced by permission of the Crown's Patentee, Cambridge University Press.

Extracts from *The Book of Prayer and Order of Service according to the Custom of the Spanish and Portuguese Jews*, are reproduced by permission of the Spanish and Portuguese Jews' Congregation's Society of Heshaim.